D1406835

THE 2:7 SERIES

COURSE 1

*"Rooted and built up in Him,
strengthened in the faith as you were taught,
and overflowing with thankfulness."*
COLOSSIANS 2:7

THE GROWING DISCIPLE

NAVPRESS ®

A MINISTRY OF THE NAVIGATORS
P.O. BOX 35001, COLORADO SPRINGS, COLORADO 80935

The Navigators is an international Christian organization. Jesus Christ gave His followers the Great Commission to go and make disciples (Matthew 28:19). The aim of The Navigators is to help fulfill that commission by multiplying laborers for Christ in every nation.

NavPress is the publishing ministry of The Navigators. NavPress publications are tools to help Christians grow. Although publications alone cannot make disciples or change lives, they can help believers learn biblical discipleship, and apply what they learn to their lives and ministries.

© 1979 by The Navigators
Revised edition © 1987
All rights reserved. No part of this publication may be reproduced in any form without written permission from NavPress,
    P.O. Box 35001, Colorado Springs, CO 80935.
ISBN 08910-91661

Unless otherwise identified, Scripture quotations are from the *Holy Bible: New International Version*. Copyright © 1973 1978, 1984, International Bible Society. Used by permission of Zondervan Bible Publishers; Other versions quoted are *The Living Bible* (LB), © 1971. Used by permission of Tyndale House Publishers, Inc., Wheaton, IL 60189, all rights reserved; and the *King James Version* (KJV).

The verses in the *Topical Memory System* are quoted in these versions: the *King James Version* (KJV); the *New American Standard Bible* (NASB), © The Lockman Foundation 1960, 1962, 1963, 1968, 1971, 1972, 1973, 1975, 1977; the *Holy Bible: New International Version* (NIV). Copyright © 1973, 1978, 1984, International Bible Society. Used by permission of Zondervan Bible Publishers; and the *Revised Standard Version of the Bible* (RSV), copyrighted 1946, 1952, © 1971, 1973.

Printed in the United States of America

12 13 14 15 16 17 18 19 20 21 22 23 24 25/99 98 97 96 95

Important

PARTICIPANTS

This course is designed to be used *only* by those who have successfully completed *Growing Strong in God's Family*. *Growing Strong in God's Family* is available from your Christian Bookstore or from NavPress.

LEADERS

Courses in *The 2:7 Series* should be *led only* by qualified leaders who have *participated in an instructor training* clinic. Clinics are available to churches and individuals desiring access to this discipleship curriculum. Information regarding training clinics may be obtained from Church Discipleship Ministries, The Navigators, P.O. Box 6000, Colorado Springs, CO 80934. The telephone number is (719) 598-1212.

Comprehensive leaders guides have been prepared for those leading groups in *The 2:7 Series*. The leaders guides are available only to those who have attended a training clinic.

ACKNOWLEDGMENT

We are grateful for the dedicated efforts of Ron Oertli who originated the concept of *Growing Strong in God's Family* and *The 2:7 Series* and is their principal author.

Contents

Bible Reading Highlights Records and Prayer sheets are included following page 89.

Completion Record

Ask others in your study group to check you on your completion of the requirements in this course and have them initial and date each section.

SCRIPTURE MEMORY	Initial	Date
Live the New Life, TMS **A** 1-12, memory verses:		
"Christ the Center"—2 Corinthians 5:17		
"Christ the Center"—Galatians 2:20		
"Obedience to Christ"—Romans 12:1		
"Obedience to Christ"—John 14:21		
"The Word"—2 Timothy 3:16		
"The Word"—Joshua 1:8		
"Prayer"—John 15:7		
"Prayer"—Philippians 4:6-7		
"Fellowship"—1 John 1:3		
"Fellowship"—Hebrews 10:24-25		
"Witnessing"—Matthew 4:19		
"Witnessing"—Romans 1:16		
Quoted all of *Live the New Life,* **A** 1-12		
Quoted all of *Beginning with Christ*		
Reviewed *Beginning with Christ* for 14 consecutive days		
Completed Scripture Memory Principles Quiz on page 15		
Completed the Self-checking Quiz on pages 36-37		

QUIET TIME		
Completed *Bible Reading Highlights Record* for 14 consecutive days		

WITNESS		
Relating activity, pages 44-45		
Testimony given from a 3" x 5" card—under four minutes		

BIBLE STUDY		
Session 2—"Maturing in Christ" (pages 15-19)		
Session 3—"Spiritual Warfare" (pages 26-29)		
Session 4—"Faith and the Truths of God" (pages 31-34)		
Session 5—"Knowing God's Will" (pages 38-43)		
Session 6—"Walking as a Servant" (pages 45-49)		

ARTICLES STUDIED	**Initial**	**Date**
Relationship Evangelism (pages 22-26)		
My Heart Christ's Home (pages 69-73)		
How to Spend a Day in Prayer (pages 77-82)		
GROUP EXERCISE		
Spent a half day in prayer		
OTHER		
Completed pages 74-75		...
LEADER'S CHECK		
Graduated from Course 1		

Session 1

OUTLINE OF THIS SESSION:
1. Go over "Review the Goals of *Growing Strong in God's Family*" (page 7).
2. Preview Course 1 by looking over the *Completion Record* (pages 5-6).
3. Survey the "Scripture Memory Instructions—Week One" (page 8).
4. Read aloud "Introduction to Bible Study—Course 1" (page 9).
5. Read and discuss "Principles for Memorizing Scripture" (pages 9-10).
6. Discuss "Practical Suggestions on Prayer" (pages 10-11). Locate Prayer sheets at the end of this book.
7. Read the "Assignment for Session 2" (page 12).
8. Close the session in prayer.

Review the Goals of Growing Strong In God's Family

The goals of *Growing Strong In God's Family* were:
1. To enjoy Bible reading by . . .
   a. using a contemporary translation or paraphrase.
   b. using a method of Bible marking.
2. To successfully memorize the five key Scripture memory verses contained in *Beginning with Christ.*
3. To experience a more consistent and meaningful quiet time by . . .
   a. combining meaningful Bible reading and prayer.
   b. succeeding in having 7 consecutive quiet times during the course.
   c. recording daily quiet time thoughts on a *Bible Reading Highlights Record.*
4. To complete and discuss *The Wheel* Bible Study as a participant in a study group.
5. To study and discuss *Tyranny of the Urgent.*
6. To become familiar with *The Wheel Illustration.*
7. To come to a deeper conviction about reasons for memorizing Scripture and to identify possible hindrances to doing well in Scripture memory.
8. To establish an Evangelism Prayer List.

Scripture Memory Instructions—Week One
From the *Topical Memory System*

You Can Memorize Scripture!

Your Memory Is Good. Do you think you have a poor memory? Wait a minute. What's your address and phone number? How about all that information you know by heart about your job? How about all the people you call by name? Or the facts and figures you can recite about your favorite sport or hobby? You see, your memory is really pretty good after all. Anything is easy to memorize when you are really interested in it, or use it often.

Attitude Makes the Difference. A good memory is not something you either have or don't have. It is a skill, and like other skills it can be improved. Attitude is what makes the difference. Adopt an attitude of confidence in Scripture memory and you will develop skill in memorizing.

Count on God's Help. Here's some additional encouragement: You can count on God to help you memorize Scripture, for He wants His Word to be in the hearts of His children. "These commandments that I give you today are to be upon your hearts" (Deuteronomy 6:6); "Let the word of Christ dwell in you richly" (Colossians 3:16).

Why the Topics?

In the TMS you will learn Bible verses according to topics—two verses for each topic. Two important reasons for knowing the topics of verses you memorize are:

1. The topics help you understand the verses, and make them easier to memorize and review.

2. The topics give you mental hooks with which to draw a particular verse from memory when you need it. They help you call the right verse to mind when witnessing, counseling, doing Bible study, or preparing a talk.

The topical outline of the course gives you the course's overall perspective and shows you where you are going. In learning anything, it helps if you first get "the big picture." Once you have the outline in mind, the topics become pegs on which to hang the verses as you learn them.

So familiarize yourself with the topical outline on page 9 and learn the topics as you learn the verses.

A Look at the Topical Memory System

The *Topical Memory System* (TMS) is designed to help you learn four things:

1. How to *memorize* Scripture verses most easily.

2. How to *apply* the verses to your life.

3. How to *review* them so you will always have them at your fingertips.

4. How to *continue* memorizing Scripture after you finish this course.

The Topical Memory System *In This Course*

The *Topical Memory System* includes 60 verses grouped into five series:

A. *Live the New Life*
B. *Proclaim Christ*
C. *Be Christ's Disciple*
D. *Grow in Christlikeness*
E. *Rely on God's Resources*

Each series has six topics and two verses for each topic, for a total of 12 verses in each series. All of the topics relate to important areas of the Christian life.

In Course 1 you will memorize the first 12 verses:

A. *Live the New Life*

Christ the Center	2 Corinthians 5:17	Galatians 2:20
Obedience to Christ	Romans 12:1	John 14:21
The Word	2 Timothy 3:16	Joshua 1:8
Prayer	John 15:7	Philippians 4:6-7
Fellowship	1 John 1:3	Hebrews 10:24-25
Witnessing	Matthew 4:19	Romans 1:16

Introduction to Bible Study—Course 1

The Bible is a book of life, a treasure chest of truth . . .

> . . . reviving the soul,
> . . . making wise the simple,
> . . . giving joy to the heart,
> . . . giving light to the eyes,
> . . . more precious than gold,
> . . . sweeter than honey . . .
> and in obeying its teachings there is great reward.
> —from Psalm 19:7-11

The abundant wisdom and riches God has provided in His Word are available to every Christian, but they are possessed only by those who diligently dig for them. Meditation and prayer are two keys which unlock this storehouse of God's wisdom as you study. Prayerfully meditating on each verse you look up will help you understand its meaning and its application for your life.

As you continue to walk with Christ, you may wonder what God's plan and purpose is for your life, how you should walk by faith, and what He desires to see in your life. During Course 1 you will be doing Bible study on five important subjects concerning your walk with Christ:

> Maturing in Christ
> Spiritual Warfare
> Faith and the Truths of God
> Knowing God's Will
> Walking as a Servant

Principles For Memorizing Scripture

AS YOU START TO MEMORIZE THE VERSE

1. Study the Scripture Memory *Instructions* each week. This material is extremely helpful and should be reviewed each week.
2. Read the *context* of the verse in your Bible. This will help you understand the setting of the verse.

3. Get a clear *understanding* of what each verse actually means. You may want to read the verse in one or two translations or paraphrases to get a better grasp of the meaning.
4. *Read* the verse through several times thoughtfully, aloud, or in a whisper. This will help you grasp the verse as a whole. Each time you read it, say the topic, reference, verse, and reference.
5. Discuss the verse with God in *prayer,* and continue to seek His help for being successful in Scripture memory.

WHILE YOU ARE MEMORIZING THE VERSE
6. Work on the verse *aloud* as often as possible.
7. Learn the topic, reference and first phrase as *one unit.*
8. After learning the topic, reference and first phrase, continue to memorize by adding an *additional* phrase after you feel comfortable in quoting correctly what you have already learned.
9. Choose a *time* when your mind is free from outside distractions. Just before retiring at night or when you first get up in the morning are excellent times for memorizing. Keep in mind whether you are a "night" or a "morning person."
10. As you memorize and review the verse, think about *how it applies* to your own life and daily circumstances.
11. Always include the *topic and reference* as a part of the verse.
12. One excellent habit to form is to use *spare moments* during the day, such as while waiting, walking or driving to review or meditate on verses.

AFTER YOU CAN SAY THE TOPIC, REFERENCE, VERSE AND REFERENCE CORRECTLY
13. It is helpful to *write* the verse out. This deepens the impression in your mind.
14. Review the verse *immediately and frequently* in the first few days after learning the verse. This is crucial for getting the verse firmly fixed in mind.
15. REVIEW! REVIEW! REVIEW! *Repetition* is the best method to deepen your impressions of verses and to maintain an ability to quote them accurately.

Practical Suggestions on Prayer

A SUGGESTED PRAYER FORMAT: *A-C-T-S*
The disciples asked Jesus to teach them how to pray (Luke 11:1-4). Jesus gave them a pattern that began with praise and adoration and ended with supplication.

One helpful way to follow this pattern is to use the acrostic *A-C-T-S,* (adoration, confession, thanksgiving, supplication).

Look up the following verses and write a summary thought for each:

Adoration: Acknowledging God's character and attributes

1 Chronicles 29:11 _____

Psalm 145:1-3 _____

Confession: Confessing your sins to God (some prefer to do this first)

     Psalm 32:5 _____

     Job 42:5-6 _____

Thanksgiving: Expressing thanks for things for which you are grateful

     Ephesians 5:20 _____

     Psalm 100:4 _____

Supplication: Asking God for things

     Matthew 7:7-8 _____

     James 4:2 _____

This prayer format is an approach you may use for a week or two and then change to another pattern. A few weeks later you may choose to return to it. It is to use as much or as little as you choose.

USE OF PRAYER SHEETS

"Devote yourselves to prayer, being watchful and thankful."
—Colossians 4:2

It is a great encouragement to see answers to prayer. Recording how God has answered them alerts us to His working and reminds us to be thankful. We can expect answers as our prayers are in line with His will (1 John 5:14, 15). Not every prayer request we pray should be written down here, but only selected ones, particularly those that have special meaning.

You can record requests that you want to bring to the Lord repeatedly. These are prayers that are important to your life, family, ministry, or job. Be specific in your prayer. Be bold. Follow the counsel in Hebrews 4:16: "Let us then approach the throne of grace with confidence, so that we may receive mercy and find grace to help us in our time of need."

Your request should be stated so that you can tell when God has answered. It is quite difficult to write a specific answer for a vague request. You should also record the date of your requests and their answers. Recording prayer answers regularly can be a stimulus to faith and more consistent prayer.

Blank Prayer sheets are included in the back of this book for your use.

A sample sheet of answers to prayer:

2/4 Floor covering for basement floor at reasonable price.	5/20 $14. carpet and pad for only $1.95/sq. yard.
2/10 Membership in the right church for us.	3/16 Confirmed that Westside church is for us.

2/13- Someone to start discipling by March 15.	5/12- George seems to be the one!
3/10- Christian friend for 10-year old Mark.	6/20- Adams family moved next door. Their son John is 12.
3/28- That Bill Alden would finish the TMS.	
4/17- To be close friends with George and Mary.	
5/4- Extra money to attend July conference.	6/8- Garage sale brought in $302.
5/10- Jerry Cole would get a job in the Middle East.	
5/11- Safe delivery and a healthy baby for Al and Nancy.	6/8 Seth Allen arrived in good health.
5/31- Close friendship with Don S.	

ASSIGNMENT FOR SESSION 2:

1. Scripture Memory: Study and complete "Scripture Memory Instructions—Week Two" (pages 13-14). Memorize the two verses on "Christ the Center," 2 Corinthians 5:17 and Galatians 2:20.

    You will take a Scripture Memory Principles Quiz during Session 2, so you will want to review the "Principles for Memorizing Scripture" (pages 9-10). In the quiz you will list at least six principles of Scripture memory. (Passing this quiz is one of the requirements for graduation from Course 1.)

2. Quiet Time: Continue your Bible reading and marking as you learned in *Growing Strong In God's Family.* Continue to use your *Bible Reading Highlights Record* and *My personal Reading Record.*

3. Bible Study: Complete the Bible study "Maturing in Christ" (pages 15-19).

4. Other:

    a. Begin using a Prayer sheet to record your requests and God's answers. You will report on this assignment in Session 4.

    b. Bring your Evangelism Prayer List to class.

    c. Finish several requirements and be ready to have them initialed on your *Completion Record.*

Session 2

OUTLINE OF THIS SESSION:

1. Break into verse review groups and review the two verses on "Christ the Center," 2 Corinthians 5:17 and Galatians 2:20. Also review the five *Beginning with Christ* verses you learned in *Growing Strong in God's Family*. (Work at getting everything signed that you can on your *Completion Record*).
2. Share your quiet time thoughts from your *Bible Reading Highlights Record.*
3. Complete the "Scripture Memory Principles Quiz" (page 15).
4. Discuss regular use of the Evangelism Prayer List.
5. Discuss the Bible study, "Maturing in Christ" (pages 15-19).
6. Read the "Assignment for Session 3" (page 20).
7. Close in prayer. Focus on people from your Evangelism Prayer List.

Scripture Memory Instructions — Week Two

And Now to Begin . . .

Each week you will have three things to work with:

1. *Your memory materials*—the verse cards and a verse pack. (Don't put all the cards in the pack at once. Keep them in a convenient place where they will be accessible each week.)

2. *Comments about the verses*—to make the verses more meaningful and easier to learn and apply.

3. *Your weekly plan*—to help you progress step by step in your memory work and avoid possible pitfalls.

About the Verses

SERIES A. LIVE THE NEW LIFE

Every person has physical life. When we have received Jesus Christ into our lives as Savior and Lord, we then possess a new, spiritual life—the life of Christ in us.

This new life may be illustrated by a wheel, as we saw in *Growing Strong in God's Family.* A wheel gets its motivating force from the hub. In the Christian life *Christ is the hub,* the source of power and motivation for living for Him (see John 15:5). He lives in us in the person of the Holy Spirit, whose expressed purpose is to glorify Christ.

The rim of the wheel represents you, the Christian, responding to Christ's lordship through your wholehearted obedience to Him. Such obedience is linked with every other element of the Christ-centered life.

The spokes of the wheel show the means by which Christ's power reaches our lives. The vertical spokes concern our relationship to God. The horizontal spokes represent our relationships to other people, both believers and unbelievers. The wheel functions smoothly only when all the spokes are present and in proper balance.

TOPIC 1. CHRIST THE CENTER

Just as the driving force in a wheel comes from the hub, so the power to live the

13

Christian life comes from Christ. It is not our resolve to "turn over a new leaf," but our active dependence on Him that enables us to live lives that are pleasing to God.

2 Corinthians 5:17—Life in Christ is completely new, and His presence gives an entirely new dimension to it. Our old ambitions, outlook, and values are changed as we come to know Him and as His power becomes operative in our lives.

Galatians 2:20—Not only are we in Christ, but He lives in us. These two truths teach us the closeness of the relationship we enjoy with Him. As believers, we are identified with Him in His death and in His resurrected life. By faith we rely on Him to live His life in and through us.

Your Weekly Plan

1. If you have not already done so, put your name, address, and phone number on the identification card from *Growing Strong in God's Family,* and put it in your verse pack for identification if you should lose the pack. Place 2 Corinthians 5:17 and Galatians 2:20 in the window on the outside of your verse pack (the widow is for the verses you are currently memorizing). Make sure 2 Corinthians 5:17 is showing.

Put the five verses from *Growing Strong in God's Family* inside the pack in one of the pockets. The verses you have learned and are currently reviewing will be kept inside the pack.

2. If your 2:7 class meets on Sunday, memorize the first verse on Monday and Tuesday. As soon as you can, say the verse at least once without looking. Then repeat it frequently throughout Monday and Tuesday to fix it firmly in mind.

3. Follow the same steps with the second verse on Wednesday and Thursday, and review the first verse. Review both verses on Friday and Saturday.

4. When you learn or review a verse, always say the topic, then the reference, then the verse, and the reference again at the end. For example, "Christ the Center, Second Corinthians five seventeen, 'Therefore, if anyone is in Christ, he is a new creation; the old has gone, the new has come!' Second Corinthians five seventeen."

5. *Note:* The capital "A" in the lower left corner of each card indicates the TMS series in which the verse is included. The number with the letter indicates the position of the verse within the series. These are not to be memorized; they are merely there to help you keep the verses in order.

6. By the end of the week, before coming to class, write out these two verses from memory or quote them to someone to make sure you have learned them correctly.

"I seek you with all my heart;
    do not let me stray from your commands.
I have hidden your word in my heart
    that I might not sin against you. . . .
I meditate on your precepts
    and consider your ways."
        —Psalm 119:10-11, 15

Scripture Memory Principles Quiz

_____

_____

_____

_____

_____

_____

_____

_____

_____

_____

_____

_____

_____

_____

_____

_____

_____

MATURING IN CHRIST

The 20th century world is characterized by rapid change. Increasingly, technological advances are providing instant communication via satellite and instant information stored and transmitted by high speed computers. We are a generation that has come to expect and demand everything "now." Christians must remember, however, that there is no such thing as "instant maturity" in the Christian experience. Becoming a Christian begins a lifelong adventure of knowing God better and loving Him more.

> *"Don't let the world around you squeeze you into its own mold, but let God re-mold your minds from within, so that you may prove in practice that the plan of God for you is good, meets all His demands and moves towards the goal of true maturity."*
>
> —Romans 12:2 PH

THINK ABOUT:

   What are some similarities between physical and spiritual development?

MOVING TOWARD MATURITY

1. You took your first step toward spiritual maturity when you put your faith in Christ. Read Ephesians 4:11-16.

   a. What is God's desire for you? Verses 13, 15

   _____

   _____

   b. What are some characteristics of immature Christians ("children" or "infants")? Verse 14

   _____

   _____

   c. According to this passage, what characterizes a spiritually mature person?

   _____

   _____

2. Contrast a person's old nature with the Christian's new nature. Ephesians 4:22-24

OLD NATURE	NEW NATURE

3. Consider 2 Corinthians 3:18.

   a. Into whose image are you being changed? _____

   b. Who brings about this change? _____

   c. How rapidly do you think change usually occurs? _____

   _____

   d. How complete will the change finally be? _____

   _____

   _____

4. What do the following verses in Romans tell you about your relationship to Christ?

   a. What has already happened to you? Romans 5:8-9 _____

   _____

b. What should you be doing now? Romans 6:19 _____

_____

_____

c. What can you expect in the future? Romans 8:16-18 _____

_____

These three aspects of salvation in Christ (justification, sanctification, glorification) are helpful in understanding God's plan for believers.

Justification	Past tense—I have been saved—from the penalty of sin.	My position is in Christ
Sanctification	Present tense—I am being saved—from the power of sin.	My condition is becoming like Christ.
Glorification	Future tense—I will be saved—from the presence of sin.	My expectation is to be like Christ.

YOUR STARTING POINT
5. Examine Colossians 2:6-7.

a. How did you begin your life in Christ? _____

_____

b. How should you continue to grow? _____

_____

6. Consider Romans 5:1-5. What foundation do we have for building a close relationship with God?

_____

_____

_____

_____

_____

7. Read Ephesians 1:1-14 and list several things which you have "in Christ."

Verse _____   _____

Verse _____   _____

Verse _____   _____

Verse _____   _____

Which of these is most important to you? Why?

_____

_____

_____

THE PROCESS OF GROWTH

8. What observations do you have about the process of spiritual growth from the following passages?

   a. 1 Peter 2:2-3

   _____

   _____

   b. Hebrews 5:13-14

   _____

   _____

   _____

9. Where do good works fit in the Christian life? Ephesians 2:8-10

   _____

   _____

   _____

As you reflect on your life, be thankful for all that God is doing in you. Take a moment to express your gratitude to God for what He has done, is doing, and will do for you.

Our outer person is merely God's frame—the real picture is the inner person which God, the Artist, is still creating.

THE MATURE LIFE

10. Who is the Christian's ultimate example? Ephesians 5:1-2

    _____

    To what extent do you think a Christian can and should imitate Christ's lifestyle?

    _____

    _____

    _____

11. What attitude should a mature Christian possess? Philippians 3:13-15

    _____

    _____

    _____

12. What are some character traits of a mature Christian? 2 Peter 1:5-7

_____

_____

_____

Describe a person without these traits. 2 Peter 1:8-11

_____

_____

_____

_____

_____

13. What impressed you most from this Bible study?

_____

_____

_____

_____

_____

_____

SUMMARY

Moving Toward Maturity

God intends Christians to mature and become like Jesus Christ. God has saved Christians from the penalty of sin. They are presently engaged in a conflict with sin, but can anticipate a future with Christ completely free from sin.

Your Starting Point

Faith in Jesus Christ marks the beginning of Christian growth. The believer has God's resources available to him to help him grow.

The Process of Growth

Spiritual growth is similar to physical growth. It takes time as God works in the believer's life.

The Mature Life

Growing in Christ is similar to walking. Following Christ's example and led by the Spirit, Christians are to walk in fellowship with Christ in faith and love. A mature Christian is one who continues to follow Christ, abounding in His work and experiencing His grace and love.

ASSIGNMENT FOR SESSION 3:

1. Scripture Memory: Study and complete "Scripture Memory Instructions—Week Three" (page 21). Memorize the two verses on "Obedience to Christ," Romans 12:1 and John 14:21.
2. Quiet Time: Continue using your *Bible Reading Highlights Records, My Personal Reading Record,* and your Prayer sheets.
3. Bible Study: Complete the Bible study, "Spiritual Warfare" (pages 26-29).
4. Other: Read and mark the article on "Relationship Evangelism," (pages 22-26) and be prepared to discuss it.

Session 3

OUTLINE OF THIS SESSION:

1. Break into verse review groups and quote the two verses on "Obedience to Christ," Romans 12:1 and John 14:21.
2. Quote the five verses learned in *Growing Strong in God's Family.*
3. Share quiet time thoughts.
4. Discuss your observations from "Relationship Evangelism" (pages 22-26).
5. Discuss the Bible study, "Spiritual Warfare" (pages 26-29).
6. Read the "Assignment for Session 4" (page 29).
7. Close in prayer.

Scripture Memory Instructions—Week Three

About the Verses

TOPIC 2. OBEDIENCE TO CHRIST

Jesus inseparably links His lordship to our obedience. "Why do you call me 'Lord, Lord,' and do not do what I say?" (Luke 6:46) By obeying His will in day-to-day living we acknowledge His authority in our lives.

Romans 12:1—This verse urges us to submit to Christ's lordship by yielding control of ourselves to Him. Since He has purchased us with the price of His own blood, this is the only reasonable thing to do. As we yield to Him and obey Him, we discover that His will for us is in every way "good, pleasing, and perfect."

John 14:21—Jesus said that obedience to His Word is the proof of our love for Him. "Whoever has my commands and obeys them, . . . loves me." But before we can keep His commands, we must have them— that is, we must know what He is saying to us in His Word. This is why His Word, which you will memorize verses on next week, is so important.

Your Weekly Plan

1. Place Romans 12:1 and John 14:21 in the window of your pack, with Romans 12:1 showing on the outside.

You have learned 2 Corinthians 5:17 and Galatians 2:20, and these cards should be placed inside the pack for regular review.

2. Each day repeat the five *Beginning with Christ* verses and the two verses you learned last week.

3. Work on your two new verses as you did in Week Two. If your 2:7 class meets on Sunday, learn the first one on Monday and Tuesday, master the second on Wednesday and Thursday, and review both on Friday and Saturday. When you have learned Romans 12:1, put the card for it inside your pack, and leave John 14:21 in the window.

4. Carry the verse pack with you at all times and use spare moments during the day for review and meditation.

5. By the end of the week, check yourself by writing out your new verses or quoting them to someone before coming to class.

Relationship Evangelism

Would you agree that most Christians are apprehensive about sharing their faith with others? While most Christians feel a responsibility to share Christ with the lost, many do not do so because of fear, lack of knowhow, or uneasiness in using canned, unnatural approaches to sharing. Can you identify with any of the following excuses?

Not my gift. "I really don't have the gift for evangelism. I leave that to people who like to confront other people."

Too nervous. "I'm basically very shy. I choke up and my hands get sweaty when I have to talk to people about . . . you know, God. I'm sure God isn't calling me to share my faith."

I just don't know enough. "I'm not a good Bible student. I just can't quote all those verses to convince people about God. Plus I couldn't possibly answer all the questions they would have."

It's not my personality. "I think you have to be the type that really loves people and is super outgoing. That's just not me."

Many Christians have overcome these excuses and discovered the joy and fruit that result from sharing their faith in Christ in the context of normal relationships with people. When there is mutual trust and respect in a relationship, the believer can easily and very effectively share his faith. Not very many Christians will volunteer for door-to-door or "cold-turkey" approaches to evangelism, but relationship evangelism is an approach in which everyone can be involved.

In his excellent book *Evangelism as a Lifestyle* (NavPress, 1980), Jim Petersen explores this approach to evangelism. Most of the material in this article is paraphrased or directly quoted from Petersen's book.

The Unreached World

"A large segment of the world's population is 'people not operating within a religious framework.' Religion is not a vital part of their existence. Their personal philosophy of life is not based on religious concepts." If asked about religion, they will give the "right" answers. But they do not base their life or actions on any of those religious concepts. "Others are totally ignorant of religious matters, even of the existence of religion. It may be difficult for most of us to imagine this, but there are population segments even in America where this is true."

"How much of the American population could be considered secularized? Recently, a *Christianity Today*—Gallup Poll of Americans over 18 found that ninety-four percent believed in God or a universal spirit who functions in their mind as God. One half of these said this belief gave them great comfort. About one fourth believed that Jesus is fully God and fully man. Forty-five percent said personal faith in Christ is the only hope of heaven."

How do we interpret these survey results? They obviously reflect a wide scattering of the gospel message. But what about those who find little or no comfort in the God they believe in? Apparently, their position is simply a belief in a God who perhaps created the world and then withdrew. They don't think of Him as One who is actively involved in the affairs of men.

"The theologian Reinhold Niebuhr warned us to 'take no satisfaction in the prevailing religiosity of our nation. Much of it is a perversion of the Christian gospel.' . . . In view of Gallup's statistics . . . and our definition of the word secular, is it not reasonable to regard half of the American population as secularized—as people not operating within a religious framework?"

Our limited success in communicating across the frontiers of different mentalities and cultures indicates that we must be overlooking some major scriptural truths in this matter of communicating the gospel to the world. Have we limited our understanding of evangelism such that we are not really communicating to the secularized?

Proclaiming and Affirming the Gospel

In order to effectively communicate the gospel, we must first understand what the Scriptures teach about evangelism. The Scriptures speak of two primary means of evangelism.

"1. The *proclamation* of the gospel: An *action* through which the non-Christian receives a clear statement of the essential message."

"2. The *affirmation* of the gospel: A *process* of modeling and explaining the Christian message."

Both proclamation and affirmation are essential if we are to evangelize those from secular backgrounds as well as those who have religious backgrounds. One cannot be judged better or more effective than the other. Both are essential, and both are limited. The New Testament pattern seems to be that they should work together.

Proclaiming the Gospel

Proclamation "is an action through which the non-Christian receives a clear statement of the gospel message. It is something that happens at a certain point in time—for example, during an evangelistic crusade, a radio or television broadcast, or a personal presentation of the gospel message to an individual. When someone declares the terms of man's reconciliation to God, the gospel has been proclaimed."

The Bible commands us to proclaim the gospel to the entire world, so whether we should engage in this is beyond discussion. Proclamation, however, must be used wisely if we expect to communicate the message to all kinds of peoples. It is effective mainly among prepared people—that is, those who have a religious heritage. Proclamation, which focuses on reaping, is most effective where sowing and watering have taken place beforehand.

Proclaiming the gospel worked well for the first missionaries in the book of Acts. "They followed a certain tactic everywhere they went. First, they visited the synagogue. Obviously, almost everyone found in a synagogue would have some spiritual interest. Although these people had not heard about Christ, they were seeking after God according to their traditional patterns. They had the benefit of a religious heritage. The result was that many of them believed when Paul and Barnabas proclaimed the gospel."

Affirming the Gospel

The affirmation of the gospel is a *process* of demonstrating the Christian message. Affirmation is carried on by modeling a Christian life-style. This Christian life-style represents new values and attitudes to the non-Christian in the context of relationships. An example of a person affirming the gospel is the hard-working Christian who is unfairly passed over in a promotion and is able to graciously accept his circumstance.

Affirmation is particularly effective among the secularized—that is, people without a Christian heritage and who do not believe that Christianity is a credible basis for their lives.

Steve, a businessman, fits into this category of secularized people. As a child, he had only limited church exposure and could not recall ever reading the Bible or talking about God at home. By the time he was 20, religion had no part in Steve's thinking.

In his early 20's Steve met and developed a friendship with Randy. They spent much time together going to movies, sporting events, and backpacking in the mountains. Randy was a Christian, but Steve noticed that he was not like other religious people he had met. *Randy accepted him* the way he was and did not criticize his life-style.

Randy asked Steve to attend church with him, and he did so on occasion. Usually Steve made fun of the sermons, but instead of becoming defensive, Randy would find some humor in Steve's remarks and laugh along with him. *Unknown to Steve, Randy faithfully prayed for his salvation.*

Five years after Steve and Randy met, Steve faced an emotional crisis. In despair, he considered ending his life, but first turned to his one true friend for help. Steve poured out his heart to Randy. *Randy listened carefully, then responded gently with the message of Jesus Christ,* explaining how Christ could meet all of Steve's needs. That night, driving home, Steve opened his heart to the Savior.

Steve had not responded positively to a presentation of the gospel message previously. However, having observed Randy as he faithfully affirmed the gospel in his life, and having been the object of faithful prayer, when a crisis arose in his life, Steve was open to the proclamation of the gospel.

Evangelism as a Process

"When we bring someone to a decision to trust in Christ in the course of a conversation or two, we can be sure of one thing: considerable preparation and laboring has already occurred in that life before we arrived on the scene. This is what Jesus was saying to the Twelve in John 4:36-38: 'The reaper draws his wages, even now he harvests the crop for eternal life, so that the sower and the reaper may be glad together. Thus the saying "One sows and another reaps" is true. I sent you to reap what you have not worked for. Others have done the hard work, and you have reaped the benefits of their labor.'

"God uses many influences to prepare a person's heart for the gospel message: people, circumstances and events.

"Some of the essential steps along the way only God can accomplish. The God-consciousness planted in the heart of every person is one of these (see Romans 1:20). God has also written His law in people's hearts, accompanying it with a conscience and sense of guilt (see Romans 2:14-15)."

Sometimes God uses job problems, broken relationships, uprooted homes, or personal tragedies that disrupt the routines and values of normal life. All of these events can serve to draw people away from the dominion of darkness and toward the Kingdom of light.

"Even chance comments can be significant. An ex-Buddhist, describing his conversion to Christ, pointed back to a comment by his mother while they were in the Buddhist temple as being the trigger that started

his search that led him to Christ. She wondered aloud why the 'true God' was positioned last, not first, on the shelf of idols in the temple. He never forgot his mother's question. Her comment prepared him to respond to the Christian gospel.

"God uses an endless variety of ways and means to sow the seed of the gospel message and move us along from ignorance and rebellion toward faith. The most obvious means, and by far the most effective, is a strong Christian family—growing up where the fundamentals of Christianity are practiced and taught in the home and church. After such an education, often the sole remaining need is reaping. People with a religious heritage still exist in significant numbers in many places. In these situations, reaping by itself produces encouraging results. This can lead us into thinking the whole world is at the same level of preparedness. It can make us forget that evangelism is, in fact, a process."

We must not be too anxious for the harvest, but we must keep in mind that before reaping come sowing, watering, and cultivating. Evangelism is not an event but a process. This process may take months, and even years.

Attitudes for Success

What attitudes are necessary to effectively affirm the gospel to non-Christians?

1. We must be willing to initiate relationships.
2. We must show the same kind of love and acceptance toward sinners that Jesus displayed.
3. We must be willing to boldly identify with Christ early in a relationship.
4. We must demonstrate dependence on God through persevering prayer.

1. *Initiate relationships.* Let us look first at the area of taking initiative in relationships. In Matthew 5:43-48, Jesus taught that we should be like our Father who causes the sun to rise on the evil and on the good. He said, "Don't just love those who love you back. Even tax collectors do that. Don't just greet your brothers. Everyone does

that. Take the initiative in being friendly and in observing what is happening among those around you."

In developing relationships with non-Christians, we need to seek rapport. "Look for the common ground. Rapport occurs when two people share common interests and/or needs. This will cost us time and privacy, but how will others see God's grace in us if we keep our distance?

"In Luke 14:12-13 Jesus suggests that when we give a dinner we shouldn't invite just our friends and relatives. You know how that goes. This time it's our turn, next time it's theirs. In the end, everyone breaks even. It hasn't cost anyone anything. Rather, He says, invite the poor, the crippled, the lame, and the blind who cannot repay you—until the day of resurrection when they will be there to salute your faithfulness to them.

"In other words, be hospitable. Deliberately break out of your daily routine of people and places for the gospel's sake."

There is perhaps no more effective environment for initiating evangelism than a dinner at home or in a quiet restaurant. We must go into the world to establish the rapport needed to draw people into our lives.

2. *Show acceptance and love.* Our attitude must be one of acceptance and love. Jesus was the friend of publicans and sinners. We must accept people as they are. Be realistic about unbelievers and don't expect too much. They are not Christians, and they will probably act accordingly. Don't come across as a reformer.

The Christian tends to measure the non-Christian against a rather legalistic list of acceptable and unacceptable behavior. The list is a mixture of clear-cut commands from the Word of God such as "Do not commit adultery," to standards that come from our traditions, such as total abstinence from alcohol.

"The non-Christian picks up the vibrations and feels he is being judged. He sometimes even apologizes for his unacceptable habits, indicating that he feels he has fallen into the hands of someone bent on reforming him. Where there are such judgments, communication is hopeless.

"Acceptance does not mean approval. The contrast between our values and theirs will become conspicuous. Be sure this contrast is based on moral and scriptural matters, not on trivial and optional things. It is our responsibility to adapt to them unless absolute moral issues are involved. Make them feel comfortable around you. Be 'all things to all men.' Remember that sanctification is a matter of the heart, not surroundings.

"Avoid judging, preaching, condemning or moralizing. 'No thank you' is definitely preferable to 'I don't smoke because I am a Christian and the Bible says. . . .' Prayer before lunch that embarasses your guest is not necessarily a good testimony! Demonstrate grace, not legalism. Be sensitive as to how your actions will affect the other person.

"Love people as they are and as individuals, not as targets for evangelism. Love. Accept. Adapt. Be a friend. . . . It has been said, 'Ninety percent of evangelism is love.'

"God's love for man is unconditional. His love is expressed through us as we commit ourselves to seeking the good of another, regardless of his response to us (1 John 3:16-18). There is an obvious link between loving and serving. If you answer the question, 'In what way can I serve this person?', you will have answered, 'How can I love him?'"

3. *Be bold.* The next attitude that is necessary for the effective affirmation of the gospel is one of boldness to be identified with Christ early in the relationship. We need to identify ourselves as Christians in the early stages, because the longer we wait without saying anything, the harder witnessing will be at a later time. If we are to be honest in relating to our non-Christian friends, it is not wise to conceal our identity as Christians. We must be open about our relationship with Christ, yet we need to guard an overly aggressive spirit that would be threatening or offensive.

One way to "run up the flag" early in the relationship is to casually interject part of your testimony when the opportunity arises. As you pray for your friend, ask God to provide the opportunity to reveal your identity as a Christian in a positive, non-threatening way. If you are faithful to do this, you will experience a more relaxed relationship, because you have been honest with your friend about who you really are. Identifying with Christ early in the relationship will also allow you to talk about spiritual things more easily later on.

4. *Depend upon God in prayer.* Finally, we must display an attitude of dependence upon God in prayer. We need to remember that the battle for souls is not a physical battle but a spiritual battle. Without wielding the weapon of prayer, we cannot expect to see God's deliverance. Not only does God want us to initiate and develop relationships, He wants us to pray faithfully for these people. "Pray your way through every step of the process, from establishing the first rapport, to opening the door to the message, to the Holy Spirit's convicting them of sin, righteousness and judgment.

"Persist in prayer (see Luke 11:9-10). George Mueller wrote, 'The great point is to never give up until that answer comes.

I have been praying every day for 52 years for two men, sons of a friend of my youth. They are not converted yet, but they will be. . . . The great fault of the children of God is that they do not persevere. If they desire anything for God's glory, they should pray until they get it.' One of these men became a Christian at George Mueller's funeral, the other some years later."

Proper attitudes are essential as we seek to affirm the gospel. First, willingness to initiate relationships will prevent us from isolating ourselves from the non-Christian world. Then, displaying love and acceptance toward sinners will enable us to manifest the grace of God and avoid the common pitfall of a legalistic and judgmental spirit. Next, boldly identifying with Christ early in the relationship will allow us to relate honestly with our non-Christian friends and will make it easier for us to discuss spiritual things later on. Finally, a commitment to depend on God will stimulate us to persist in daily prayer for those non-Christian friends God has given to us.

SPIRITUAL WARFARE

To discover and apply the great truth of God's Word is to enter the field of spiritual warfare. A battle rages for the hearts and minds of men and women. But growth comes with conflict, and God has promised that "in all these things we are more than conquerors through him who loved us" (Romans 8:37).

THINK ABOUT:
   What elements in military conflict are also true in spiritual warfare?

THE BATTLE
1. Read 2 Timothy 2:3-4. How would you describe the kind of life Paul wrote about?

_____

_____

2. How is the Christian life described by the Apostle Paul in Ephesians 6:12?

_____

_____

_____

3. How did Satan discredit God's Word when he deceived Eve? Genesis 3:1-5

_____

_____

_____

Satan makes it his continual business to cast doubt on God's Word, and to discredit God's Son.

4. What can be learned about our enemy Satan in the following verses?

Luke 8:12 _____

_____

_____

John 8:44 _____

_____

_____

2 Corinthians 4:3-4 _____

_____

_____

2 Corinthians 11:3 _____

_____

_____

2 Corinthians 11:14 _____

_____

_____

5. Read the account of Christ's confrontation with Satan in Luke 4:1-13.

a. What was Jesus' condition when the Devil appeared?

_____

_____

b. To what desires did Satan appeal in the three temptations?

_____

_____

THE OPPOSITION

We receive opposition from 3 sources: the world, the flesh and the Devil.

6. From the following passages, what characterizes the world, the flesh and the Devil?

| John 15:18-19 | James 4:1-4 | 1 Peter 5:8-9 |
| Ephesians 2:1-3 | John 8:44 | Colossians 2:8 |

THE WORLD.

Verse _____ _____

Verse _____ _____

THE FLESH.

Verse _____ _____

Verse _____ _____

THE DEVIL.

Verse _____ _____

Verse _____ _____

THE VICTORY HAS BEEN PROVIDED

OVER THE WORLD

7. What is the basis for victory over the world from the following verses?

a. 1 John 5:4-5 _____

b. John 17:14-18 _____

c. Colossians 2:6-8 _____

OVER THE FLESH

8. How do we have victory over the flesh in the following passages?

a. Ephesians 4:22-24 _____

_____

_____

b. Galatians 5:16-17 _____

_____

_____

c. Romans 6:12-13 _____

_____

_____

"Let no man think that he can have any measure of victory over his inner corruption without taking it to the Lord again and again in prayer."

—George Mueller

OVER THE DEVIL

9. According to Hebrews 2:14-15, what did Christ's death on the cross mean for Satan?

_____

_____

What does it mean for us today? _____

_____

10. Write out 1 Corinthians 15:57 in your own words as a personal prayer. Take a moment to thank God for your assurance of daily victory in Jesus Christ.

_____

_____

_____

_____

SUMMARY

The Battle
All Christians are involved in a spiritual battle between God and the forces of evil. Satan is the major adversary of God and people.

The Opposition
The Christian has three very real enemies in the spiritual battle: the world, the flesh, and the Devil.

The Victory Has Been Provided
The battle has already been won in Christ. Victory over the world, the flesh, and the Devil is assured through Christ and through His life in us.

ASSIGNMENT FOR SESSION 4:
1. Scripture Memory: Study and complete Scripture Memory Instructions—Week Four (page 30). Memorize the two verses on "The Word," 2 Timothy 3:16 and Joshua 1:8.
2. Quiet Time: Continue reading, marking, and recording.
3. Bible Study: Complete the Bible study, "Faith and the Truths of God" (pages 31-34).
4. Other: Bring your Prayer sheets with you to class.

Session 4

OUTLINE OF THIS SESSION:

1. Break into verse review groups and quote the two verses on "The Word," 2 Timothy 3:16 and Joshua 1:8.
2. Share quiet time thoughts from your *Bible Reading Highlights Record.*
3. Share results from using your Prayer sheets.
4. Discuss the Bible study, "Faith and the Truths of God," (pages 31-34).
5. Read the "Assignment for Session 5" (page 35).
6. Have a period of conversational prayer.

Scripture Memory Instructions — Week Four

About the Verses

TOPIC 3. THE WORD

The Bible in a practical sense is the foundation of the Christian life, since all we know about Jesus Christ, the true Foundation, we learn from the Bible.

2 Timothy 3:16—This verse tells us that all Scripture is inspired by God (literally, God-breathed). Peter put it this way: "Men spoke from God as they were carried along by the Holy Spirit" (2 Peter 1:21). The Scriptures are given to teach, reprove, correct, and train us in righteous living. God did not give us His Word primarily to increase our knowledge, but to govern our conduct.

Joshua 1:8—This verse promises that those who do what God's Word says will prosper. And the first step to applying His Word is to meditate on it constantly, mulling it over in our minds. Develop the habit of meditating on the passages you already know.

Your Weekly Plan

1. Place 2 Timothy 3:16 and Joshua 1:8 in the window of your pack, with 2 Timothy 3:16 showing on the outside. The cards for Romans 12:1 and Galatians 2:20 should be inside the pack for regular review.

2. Each day review the verses you have already learned and work on the two new ones. Learn the first one well, before concentrating on the second.

3. You can speed the learning process by thoughtfully writing out a new verse as you begin to work on it.

4. Always say the topic first, then the reference, the verse, and the reference again.

5. Remember, the best time to learn a new verse is either just before going to bed or just after getting up in the morning.

6. By the end of the week write out your two new verses or quote them to someone before coming to class.

FAITH AND THE TRUTHS OF GOD

A group of people once asked Jesus how they could do the work of God. Jesus replied, "The work of God is this: to believe in the one he has sent" (John 6:29). God desires belief and faith from individuals, for "without faith it is impossible to please God" (Hebrews 11:6).

But often in modern society faith is nothing more than wishful thinking—"I hope everything works out all right. I have 'faith' that it will." The biblical concept of faith far surpasses this superficial approach and is a vital necessity for walking with Christ.

THINK ABOUT:
   What do you think the following illustration is attempting to communicate?

WALKING BY FAITH

1. How would you define faith from:

Acts 27:25 _____

_____

Romans 4:20-21 _____

_____

_____

Hebrews 11:1 _____

_____

"Faith is the assurance that the thing which God has said in His Word is true, and that God will act according to what He has said in His Word. . . . Faith is not a matter of impressions, nor of probabilities, nor of appearances."

—George Mueller

The opposite of faith is not doubt; it is unbelief. Doubt only needs more facts. Unbelief is disobedience and refuses to act in accordance with what God has declared.

OBJECTS OF FAITH

2. What are some of the unworthy objects in which people may place their faith?

_____ Psalm 1:1 _____

_____ Psalm 33:16-17 _____

_____ Proverbs 3:5 _____

_____ Jeremiah 9:23-24 _____

Place an "x" by those on which you find yourself most likely to depend.

What do you feel is the inevitable result of placing faith in these objects?

_____

_____

_____

_____

_____

_____

_____

_____

3. God makes and fulfills promises. What do the following passages teach about God?

1 Kings 8:56 _____

_____

Psalm 89:34 _____

_____

2 Peter 1:4 _____

_____

Numbers 23:19 _____

_____

"Faith always attaches itself to what God has said or promised. When an honorable man says anything, he also does it; on the back of the saying follows the doing. So also it is with God; when He would do anything, He says so first in His Word."

—Andrew Murray

EXAMPLES OF FAITH

4. Read Hebrews 11 and list at least three things which impress you.

_____

_____

_____

_____

_____

_____

TRUTHS YOU CAN TRUST

5. Fill in the following chart.

VERSE	TRUTH	CONDITION, IF ANY
John 15:7		
Isaiah 26:3		
Romans 8:28-29		

> _"How to Handle the Bible:_
> _—Get everything out of it._
> _—Do not read anything into it._
> _—Let nothing remain unread in it."_
> —J.A. Bengel

6. Why do you feel God places conditions on some promises?

_____

_____

What should your attitude be toward God's promises? Hebrews 6:12

_____

_____

_____

_____

_____

_____

It is helpful and encouraging to note God's promises. You may want to keep a list of these promises, their conditions, and their results. God's promises often form a "chain" like the following example.

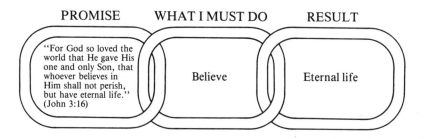

7. What is one promise you have discovered in your Bible reading?

_____

_____

_____

Specifically, how has this promise helped you? _____

_____

_____

SUMMARY

Walking by Faith
Faith is based on the certain Word of God. Believing God and His Word gives the Christian the experience of hope, joy, peace, answered prayer, and the fulfillment of many other promises of God.

Objects of Faith
People may entrust their lives to a number of things which will ultimately fail. Only God and His Word are worthy of our complete trust.

Examples of Faith
Many men and women throughout history have believed God and trusted Him. Hebrews 11 is a hall of fame list of some of those people.

Truths You Can Trust
Promises often have conditions. This is true of God's promises. We must not be careless or presumptuous in handling His Word.

ASSIGNMENT FOR SESSION 5:

1. Scripture Memory: Study and complete "Scripture Memory Instructions—Week Five" (page 36). Memorize the first verse on "Prayer," John 15:7. Take the Self-checking Quiz on pages 36-37.
2. Quiet Time: Continue reading, marking, recording and using your Prayer sheets.
3. Bible Study: Complete the Bible study, "Knowing God's Will" (pages 38-43).

Session 5

OUTLINE OF THIS SESSION:
1. Break into verse review groups and quote the first verse on "Prayer," John 15:7. (Work at getting everything signed that you can on your *Completion Record.*)
2. Briefly discuss the "Self-checking Quiz" on pages 36-37.
3. Share your quiet time thoughts from your *Bible Reading Highlights Records.*
4. Discuss the Bible study, "Knowing God's Will" (pages 38-43).
5. Read the "Assignment for Session 6" (page 43).
6. Close in prayer. Focus on people from your Evangelism Prayer List.

Scripture Memory Instructions — Week Five

About the Verses

TOPIC 4. PRAYER

Direct communication with our heavenly Father is one of the greatest privileges the child of God has. We are urged to come confidently to God in prayer, especially in time of need (see Hebrews 4:16).

John 15:7 — This verse presents two conditions for receiving what we ask in prayer. First, we must abide in Christ, that is, we must maintain unbroken fellowship with Him. Second, we must allow His Word to abide in us, keeping it in our thoughts so it will direct our lives.

Your Weekly Plan

1. Follow the same plan as in previous weeks, adding John 15:7 and Philippians 4:6-7 to the window of your pack. You will learn only John 15:7 this week.

2. As you review your verses, look only at the topic, or the topic and the reference. Don't glance at the first words of the verse as this "help" will actually hinder your later recall of the verse.

3. Write out your new verse by the end of the week or quote it to someone to be sure you have learned it correctly.

4. Take the "Self-checking Quiz."

Self-checking Quiz

After you re-read the "Scripture Memory Instructions" for Weeks One through Five, this quiz will help you check your grasp of Scripture memory principles. Correct answers appear at the end of the quiz on page 37.

1. Memorizing Scripture is nourishment for your soul and is like stocking the pantry of your heart for future needs.
T   F   (Circle **T** for true or **F** for false.)

2. Match the following. Write the number of the correct answer in the blank space before each statement to complete it.

(1) helps you understand the verses in their setting and makes them more meaningful and easier to remember and use.
(2) makes it possible for you to use spare moments for review and meditation.
(3) gives you "the big picture" and shows you where you are going in Scripture memory.
(4) helps you progress step by step in your memory work and avoid possible pitfalls.
(5) hinders your ability to recall the verse later.
(6) helps you remember where the verses are located in the Bible.
(7) helps you speed the learning process.
(8) should be placed inside your verse pack.

_____ a. It is important to follow carefully *Your Weekly Plan* instruction section, because it . . .
_____ b. Reading the *About the Verses* comments and looking up the context in your Bible . . .
_____ c. The verses you have already learned . . .
_____ d. The principle of saying the reference before and after the verse . . .
_____ e. Becoming familiar with the topical outline of the course before learning the verses . . .
_____ f. Writing out a verse you are memorizing . . .
_____ g. Carrying your verse pack with you at all times . . .
_____ h. When reviewing, you should not glance at the first words of the verse, as this . . .

3. Why is it important that you have clearly in mind *your own reasons* for memorizing Scripture? (Check the correct answer.)
_____ a. So you can check them off when these goals have been reached.
_____ b. So you will take pride in your memory work.
_____ c. So these reasons will motivate you and help you succeed.

4. It is best to learn the verses word-perfectly because this . . . (Check three correct answers.)
_____ a. teaches you to observe details.
_____ b. makes a clearer impression on your mind so that the verses are easier to recall.
_____ c. makes your review easier.
_____ d. impresses others with your knowledge of Scripture.
_____ e. gives you confidence in using your verses.

5. Why is it recommended that you learn only one or two verses a week? (Check three correct answers.)
_____ a. To give you ample opportunity to look up the context of the verses.
_____ b. To keep you from getting through the course too quickly.
_____ c. To give you time to meditate on the verses and apply them to your life.
_____ d. To help you develop good memory habits and succeed in Scripture memory.
_____ e. To give you the scientifically proven optimum rate of learning.

6. An excellent way to get an early start on your daily memory work is to include it as a part of your morning quiet time.
T F

7. The verses in Series A deal with the essential elements of the obedient, Christ-centered life.
T F

Correct answers:

1-T; 2—a-4, b-1, c-8, d-6, e-3, f-7, g-2, h-5; 3-c; 4-b,c,e; 5-a,c,d; 6-T; 7-T.

KNOWING GOD'S WILL

Christians often wonder what God wants them to do concerning their desires and plans. It seems as though God's will is hidden in a buried treasure chest and we have only small portions of the map to find its location. But is this true? Is God keeping His plans from you as some hidden secret, or is He interested in having you follow Him so that He can lead you step by step?

A passage of Scripture that deals with this area is Proverbs 3:5-6, which you memorized in *Growing Strong in God's Family.* Quote that passage right now. Check the box after you quote it.   ☐

THINK ABOUT:
   To what extent can someone else determine God's will for your life?

GOD'S WILL

1. What should be your goals as a follower of Christ? Ephesians 5:15-17

   _____

   _____

   _____

2. What would God like to do for you? Psalm 32:8

   _____

   _____

3. What is the Holy Spirit's role? Romans 8:14

   _____

   _____

"The will of God is not like a magic package let down from heaven by a string . . . The will of God is far more like a scroll that unrolls every day . . . the will of God is something to be discerned and lived out every day of our lives. It is not something to be grasped as a package once for all. Our call, therefore, is basically not to follow a plan or a blueprint, or go to a place or take up a work, but rather to follow the Lord Jesus Christ."

—Paul Little

In the Scriptures, Christians have all the guidance they need in order to live for Jesus Christ. However, there are certain specific decisions which must be made even though the Bible does not give specific instructions. In these cases, a Christian should apply the *principles* which are contained in God's Word.

GUIDANCE PRINCIPLES

Objectives from God's Word

God has given particular commandments which can provide guidance concerning your activities. If a particular course of action is inconsistent with God's Word, then you know that it is not His will for you.

4. Using the following verses, state in your own words some of God's objectives for you. God wants you to . . .

Matthew 6:33 _____

Matthew 22:37-39 _____

Matthew 28:18-20 _____

1 Peter 1:15 _____

2 Peter 3:18 _____

1 Thessalonians 5:18 _____

Ask yourself some questions based on these and similar verses to determine your course of action:

a. Am I putting God's desire ahead of my own?

b. Will it help me to love God and others more?

c. How does this action relate to my personal involvement in fulfilling Christ's Great Commission?

d. Will this help me lead a more holy life?

e. Will this course of action increase my personal knowledge of Christ?

f. Can I be thankful whatever the results, or however it works out?

Honestly answering these questions will help you make a decision that is in accordance with God's Word.

5. Using the following verses, develop questions that will help you discern God's will.

1 Corinthians 6:12 _____

1 Corinthians 6:19-20 _____

1 Corinthians 8:9 _____

1 Corinthians 10:31 _____

Obedience to God

If you refuse to obey God in what He has already shown you, will God give you further direction? Obedience to the known will of God is important in receiving further guidance.

6. What other action can you take to learn God's will?

Psalm 143:8 _____

James 1:5 _____

7. What conditions are given in Romans 12:1-2 for finding God's will?

_____

_____

_____

8. Read Psalm 27:14 and Isaiah 30:18. How does "waiting on the Lord" relate to knowing God's will? How do you do it?

_____

_____

_____

_____

_____

Satan rushes people—God guides them.

Openness to God's Leading

Many difficulties in determining the Lord's will are overcome when you are ready to do His will, whatever it may be.

9. You may not always know all of the possible alternatives in determining what to do. What is a means by which you can gather additional information? Proverbs 15:22.

_____

10. Read Psalm 1:1

   a. Of what counsel should we be skeptical?

   _____

   _____

   b. When is it valid to seek a non-Christian's advice?

   _____

   _____

Counsel should be obtained from mature Christians who themselves are committed to the will of God and know you well. It helps to talk with others who have previously made decisions in matters you are presently experiencing.

11. What are some other considerations which can help you discern God's leading? Match the following verses with the appropriate factors.

   _____ Careful and wise thinking   a. 2 Corinthians 2:12-13

   _____ Inner spiritual peace   b. Philippians 1:12-14

   _____ Particular circumstances   c. Ephesians 5:15-17

What possible dangers exist in relying only on these factors?

_____

_____

_____

PRINCIPLES IN PRACTICE

12. Some passages in the Bible illustrate elements which affect sound judgment. Study the following examples. What was the influencing factor in making either the right or wrong decision?

PERSON	PASSAGE	ISSUE
Gideon	Judges 6:36-38	_____
		_____
Moses	Hebrews 11:25-26	_____
		_____
Demas	2 Timothy 4:10	_____
		_____

13. The following chart may be helpful in determining God's will for most decisions you face. To help you become familiar with this approach, use the chart to determine God's will for a particular decision you now face.

Decision I am facing: _____

_____

OBJECTIVES IN LIVING	YES	NO	NEUTRAL
Am I putting God's desire ahead of my own?			
Will it help me to love God and others more?			
Will it help me to fulfill the Great Commission?			
Will it help me lead a more holy life?			
Will it help me further my Christian training?			

Other questions: _____

_____

_____

_____

OBEDIENCE TO GOD

What factors from God's Word affect this decision? _____

_____

_____

_____

_____

OPENNESS TO GOD'S LEADING

ALTERNATIVES	ADVANTAGES	DISADVANTAGES
_____	_____	_____
_____	_____	_____
_____	_____	_____
_____	_____	_____
_____	_____	_____
_____	_____	_____

Counsel from mature Christians who know me well: _____

_____

_____

_____

Inner peace factor: _____

_____

_____

Circumstances: _____

_____

_____

_____

14. After prayerfully considering the above factors, my decision is: _____

_____

_____

SUMMARY

God's Will
God desires that we live productive, fulfilled lives. One reason He has given us the Scriptures is so that we might know both His specific directives and broad principles for living.

Guidance Principles
If we are to walk in God's will we need to be pursuing scriptural objectives and, with the Holy Spirit's help, be obeying God's known will. We need to want what God wants.

Principles in Practice
When making relatively significant decisions it is wise to use a checklist of factors that need to be considered. These factors should include objectives, obedience, openness, counsel, peace, and circumstances.

ASSIGNMENT FOR SESSION 6:
1. Scripture Memory: Study and complete "Scripture Memory Instructions—Week Six" (page 44). Memorize the second verse on "Prayer," Philippians 4:6-7.
2. Quiet Time: Continue reading, marking, and recording.
3. Bible Study: Complete the Bible study, "Walking as a Servant," (pages 45-49).
4. Other: Work on getting everything completed that you can on your *Completion Record*.

Session 6

OUTLINE OF THIS SESSION:
1. Break into verse review groups and quote the second verse on "Prayer," Philippians 4:6-7. (Work at getting everything signed that you can on your *Completion Record.*)
2. Share some of your quiet time thoughts from your *Bible Reading Highlights Record.*
3. Read and discuss "Developing a Relationship with a Non-Christian" (pages 44-45).
4. Discuss the Bible study, "Walking as a Servant" (pages 45-49).
5. Discuss a tentative time and place for Session 8.
6. Read the "Assignment for Session 7" (page 49).
7. Close in prayer. Pray concerning activities relating to non-Christians.

Scripture Memory Instructions — Week Six

About the Verse
TOPIC 4. PRAYER

God's antidote for worry is prayer. None of your concerns are too small or mundane to pray about.

Philippians 4:6-7 — It is a specific kind of praying that God wants: prayer with thanksgiving. Learn to thank God for everything — difficulties as well as blessings — as you overcome anxiety by prayer.

The late Dr. Ole Hallesby, Norwegian seminary professor, gives the following encouraging words in his book, *Prayer*: "My helpless friend, your helplessness is the most powerful plea which rises up to the tender father-heart of God. He has heard your prayer from the very first moment that you honestly cried to Him in your need, and night and day He inclines His ear toward earth in order to ascertain if any of the helpless children of men are turning to Him in their distress.

"Be not anxious because of your helplessness. Above all, do not let it prevent you from praying. Helplessness is the real secret and the impelling power of prayer."

Your Weekly Plan
1. Put John 15:7 inside your pack with the other verses to be reviewed, and keep Philippians 4:6-7 in the window.
2. Remember to use spare moments during the day to review and meditate.
3. Write out your new verse by the end of the week or quote it to someone to be sure you have learned it correctly.

Developing a Relationship with a Non-Christian

A part of your evangelism assignment in this course is to have an activity with a non-Christian. The purpose of this activity is to develop the friendship of the non-Christian. Of course one activity will not make a friend of a person but it is part of the process. If possible, plan a second activity. Pray that the relationship will develop.

The activity you choose should be a natural thing that you can do together. It could be as simple as having a cup of coffee together. Some other ideas you might consider are:

—Engaging in a sports activity
—Helping them on a project or serving them in some way
—Being alert for emergencies
—Going shopping together
—Inviting them over for a table game and dessert

The list is almost endless but not all activities will fit your situation.

For many believers, it is very natural to have activities with non-Christians. These times together deepen the friendship and can lead to reaching them for Christ. But many Christians have very few non-Christian *friends*.

Jesus spent so much time with non-Christians that He was called "a friend of sinners" (Matthew 11:18-19). Jesus took the initiative to seek out the lost.

Choose to be where they are. Be outside when neighbors are. Have a barbeque and invite the neighbors. Join a club. Seek them out at coffee and lunch breaks.

Be friendly and conversant. Talk about what they are interested in. Smile. Remember their name and use it when you see them. Avoid controversial topics until the relationship is quite well established.

Remember, your goal is to be *with* the non-Christian so that in time they will move from being an "acquaintance" to being a "friend." This will take time. Keep in mind that *evangelism is a process* and not an event. As the friendship develops, the foundation is being laid for sharing your faith in Christ.

WALKING AS A SERVANT

Serving is one of the greatest challenges in the life of a disciple. Everyone enjoys being served, but few make an effort to serve others. People don't mind being called servants, but they don't want to be treated as servants. The mature Christian is marked by what he will do for others without expecting anything in return.

THINK ABOUT:
Jesus was the Creator of the universe yet the supreme example of a servant. If He was a 20th century man, how do you think He would demonstrate his servanthood?

CHRIST YOUR EXAMPLE
1. What was Christ's purpose in coming to this world? Mark 10:45

2. Read John 13:1-17.

    a. How did Jesus serve the disciples? _____

    _____

    b. Why was Jesus able to give so freely of Himself? Verse 3 _____

    _____

    c. List several lessons you can learn from Christ's example in this passage.

    _____

    _____

    _____

    _____

"The Son of God became the servant of God in order to fulfill the mission of God."
—J. Oswald Sanders

3. How should we be like Christ? Phillipians 2:5-8

_____

_____

4. Who are some of the people who gladly bore the title servant?

Exodus 14:31 _____

1 Samuel 1:11 _____

1 Samuel 3:9 _____

1 Samuel 29:3 _____

Luke 1:38 _____

Philippians 1:1 _____

1 Corinthians 4:1 _____

5. What perspective did Paul have on being a servant? 1 Corinthians 4:1-5

_____

_____

_____

CHRIST'S DESIRE FOR YOU

6. What qualifications determined who would serve? Acts 6:1-7

_____

_____

_____

7. How does having an attitude of humility affect how you relate to others?
Philippians 2:3-4

_____

_____

_____

GIVING OF YOURSELF

8. What are some reasons why serving is difficult? Luke 22:24-27

_____

_____

_____

9. Read Galatians 5:13-15; 6:9-10

a. What can hold us back from serving others to our fullest capacity?

_____

_____

_____

b. What can motivate us to serve others in spite of hindrances?

_____

_____

_____

c. What is one hindrance to your serving others?

_____

_____

_____

Christians have been set free in Christ—not to do whatever they please, but to serve.
Believers have been—

> Set free from sin, to serve righteousness (Romans 6:18-19).
> Set free from Satan to serve God (1 Peter 2:16).
> Set free from self to serve others (Galatians 5:13).

Christians are no longer under obligation to serve the things of the old life, but free
to serve voluntarily the things of the new life.

10. Who did Paul serve? Why?

1 Corinthians 9:19 _____

_____

2 Corinthians 4:5 _____

_____

11. Read Proverbs 3:27 and 1 John 3:17. What do these verses tell you to do?

_____

_____

_____

_____

With what common needs could you help another person or family?

_____

_____

_____

12. In what ways can you serve others?
Romans 14:19 _____

_____

Ephesians 4:32 _____

_____

1 Thessalonians 5:11 _____

_____

James 5:16 _____

_____

1 John 3:11 _____

13. As a servant you could become proud of your serving. What are some guidelines to keep you from becoming proud? Luke 17:7-10

_____

_____

_____

_____

SUMMARY

Christ Your Example
Jesus Christ was not obligated to become a servant, He did so voluntarily. While on earth, Jesus served people in a variety of ways, giving of Himself to meet people's needs.

Christ's Desire for You
Like Christ, we should be servants to others. Having an attitude of humility enables one to serve well.

Giving of Yourself

We need to overcome hindrances to serving and be active in meeting some of the needs of others. There are many practical ways in which we can be servants.

ASSIGNMENT FOR SESSION 7:

1. Scripture Memory: Study and complete "Scripture Memory Instructions—Week Seven" (page 50). Memorize the first verse on "Fellowship," 1 John 1:3.
2. Quite Time: Continue reading, marking, and recording.
3. Personal Testimony:
   a. Study the personal testimony information on pages 51-58.
   b. Fill out one of the three testimony worksheets on pages 59-64.
4. Other: Work on getting everything completed that you can on your *Completion Record.*

Session 7

OUTLINE OF THIS SESSION:

1. Break into verse review groups and quote the first verse on "Fellowship," 1 John 1:3. (Work at getting more items completed and signed on your *Completion Record.*)
2. Read "Congratulations" (page 51).
3. Discuss the material on personal testimony preparation:
   a. "Why Prepare a Personal Testimony" (page 51).
   b. "Preparing a Personal Testimony: General Comments" (pages 51-53).
   c. "The Grape Illustration" (page 52).
   d. "Effective Personal Testimony Preparation" (pages 53-55).
   e. "Choose Your Testimony Format—Samples/Worksheets" (pages 55-64).
4. Read "Workshop Outline For Session 8" (page 65).
5. Finalize the time and place for Session 8.
6. Discuss a tentative time and place for Session 11.
7. Read the "Assignment for Session 8" (page 65).
8. Close in prayer. Focus on people from your Evangelism Prayer List and any upcoming "relating activity."

Scripture Memory Instructions — Week Seven

About the Verses

TOPIC 5. FELLOWSHIP

The Christian who is obedient to Christ will actively seek fellowship with other believers—individually, in small groups, and in the church. As members of one body, we depend on one another. You are discovering in your 2:7 group the valuable contribution to your life that other believers can make. This is according to God's design: "Now you are the body of Christ, and each one of you is a part of it" (1 Corinthians 12:27); "You are . . . fellow citizens with God's people and members of God's household (Ephesians 2:19).

1 John 1:3—This verse explains that true Christian fellowship is centered around Christ and is more than just socializing. He Himself is present with us when we get together with other believers for such fellowship.

Your Weekly Plan

1. Place 1 John 1:3 and Hebrews 10:24-25 in the window of your pack. You will learn 1 John 1:3 this week, and Hebrews 10:24-25 next week.

2. Continue a daily review of the verses in the inside sections of your pack.

3. Keep your memory habits sharp by learning the topics and references with the verses and by learning them word-perfectly. Use your spare moments for review and meditation.

Congratulations!

You are to be commended for your perseverence in completing *Growing Strong In God's Family* and proceeding successfully to this point in Course 1 of *The 2:7 Series*. The Lord has helped you reach some difficult and meaningful milestones in your spiritual growth and maturity. By God's grace you will soon be a graduate of Course 1, walking closer to God and being better prepared to serve Him wherever He wants to use you.

Why Prepare a Personal Testimony?

The Apostle Peter challenges us: "Always be prepared to give an answer to everyone who asks you to give the reason for the hope that you have" (1 Peter 3:15).

One of the most effective tools you have for sharing your faith is the story of how Jesus Christ gave you eternal life and how He has enriched your life. The Apostle John wrote, "We proclaim to you what we have seen and heard" (1 John 1:3). John was testifying about his relationship to Jesus Christ.

When the Apostle Paul stood before King Agrippa (Acts 26), he spoke simply, logically, and clearly about his life *before* salvation, *how* he met Christ, and what his life was like *after* conversion. Paul's testimony takes three or four minutes to read aloud in a conversational manner.

Although you will be writing your testimony, the purpose is not to memorize it and give it verbatim. The purpose is to help you put into words some of the important and interesting details of your conversion. The choice of the right words, the flow of your story, and knowing how to begin and how to end are all important.

As you begin this project, ask the Lord for wisdom and insight into just how to share your story. Be open to suggestions from your instructor.

Many graduates of *The 2:7 Series* have said that the work on the testimony was one of the most beneficial parts of their discipleship training. Many have come to Christ simply because people like you have sharpened their testimony while in *The 2:7 Series*. It is one way to "be prepared to give an answer to everyone who asks you to give the reason for the hope that you have."

Trust God and work hard. Give time, thought, and prayer to this important part of your training in discipleship.

Preparing a Personal Testimony: General Comments

You will be able to complete all or almost all of your testimony work by the end of the special three-to-four-hour workshop during Session 8. Some time will be given in Session 9 for sharing completed testimonies and finishing up the few testimonies not completed during Session 8.

1. PRIMARY AIM
The primary aim is for you to complete and present your personal salvation testimony from an outline on a 3x5 card.

The Grape Illustration

(VARIOUS TYPES OF TESTIMONIES ONE CAN
ACCUMULATE THROUGH
CHRISTIAN EXPERIENCE.)

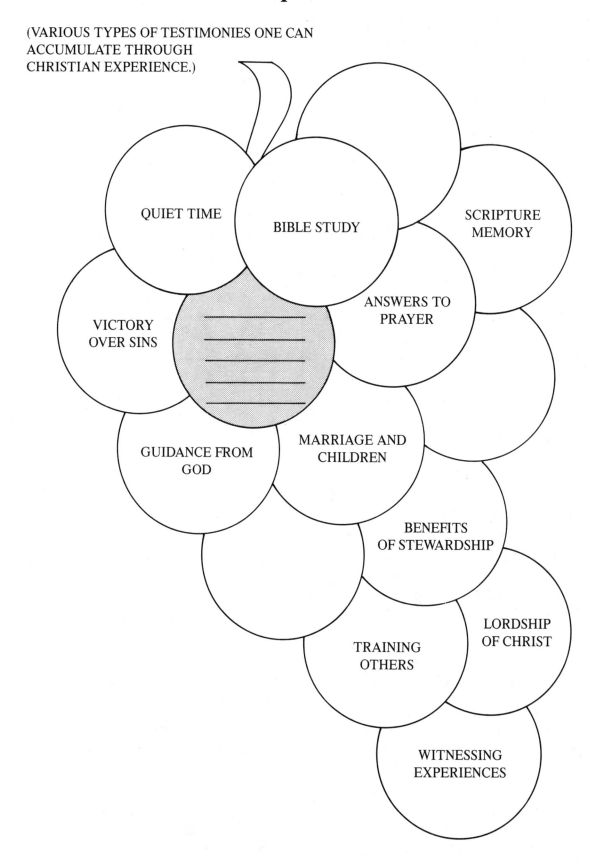

2. NUMBER OF DRAFTS

The amount of time and effort it will take each person to prepare a personal testimony may vary greatly. This has little to do with intelligence or spirituality. It has everything to do with the complexity of your story. Some testimonies are extremely difficult to communicate clearly. Some have to be condensed. Others need to be expanded. So, there are many factors which influence how long it will take you to complete your written personal testimony.

3. DIFFICULT BUT REWARDING

Some students find this work on the personal testimony the most difficult part of the course, and sometimes the most discouraging. On the other hand, many students find it to be the most profitable and stimulating part of the course. Your attitude and how aggressively you do your work can make all the difference. Work hard! Pray for God's wisdom and guidance.

4. SALVATION TESTIMONY

Testimonies can be prepared on many subjects and tailored to various audiences. The testimony you will prepare during this course . . .
- will be designed to give to a non-Christian.
- will be best suited for sharing one-on-one or in a small group.
- will primarily serve as a "door opener," not a "convincing tool."

Many people are not ready to be convinced that they need Christ, but can often be led to talk about the gospel after an inoffensive presentation of a personal testimony.

Effective Personal Testimony Preparation

OUTLINE FOR A PERSONAL TESTIMONY

Paul's testimony in Acts 26 is a biblical model you can follow in writing your own personal testimony. Paul's format in Acts 26 is:

Lead-In	Verses 2-3
BEFORE	Verses 4-11
HOW	Verses 12-20
AFTER	Verses 21-23
Close	Verses 24-29

During Sessions 7 and 8 you will prepare only a *before, how* and *after.* The *lead-in* and *close* that you use will vary with each person and situation. The *lead-in* and *close* will be discussed in Session 9.

GUIDELINES FOR PREPARING THE MORE SPECIFIC CONTENT

1. *Make it sound conversational.* Avoid literary sounding statements. Use informal language.

2. *Share, don't preach. Say "I" and "me," not "you."* This helps keep the testimony warm and personal.

3. *Avoid religious words, phrases, and jargon.*

RELIGIOUS WORDS	POSSIBLE SUBSTITUTES
Believe/Accepted Christ	Trusted or relied on Christ for my salvation
Sin	Disobedience, breaking God's laws, turned my back on God
Went forward	Decided to turn my life over to God
Under the blood	God forgave the wrongs I had done
Saved/Born Again	Became a real Christian
Christian	Committed Christian, real Christian

4. *Generalize so more people can identify with your story.* Don't name specific churches, denominations, or groups. Avoid using dates and ages.

5. *Include some humor and human interest.* When a person smiles or laughs, it reduces tension. Humor is disarming and increases attention.

6. *One or two word pictures increase interest.* Don't just say, "Bill shared the gospel with me." You might briefly describe the setting so a person listening can visualize it.

7. Explain how Christ met or is meeting your deep inner needs, but *do not communicate that all your struggles and problems ended at conversion.*

8. *Sound adult, not juvenile.* Reflect an adult point of view even if you were converted at an early age.

9. *Avoid dogmatic and mystical statements which skeptics can question,* such as, "I prayed and God gave me a job," or "God said to me."

10. *Simplify—reduce "clutter."* Mention a limited number of people and use only their first or last names. Combine information when you can.
    a. Poor: "Martha Smith, Nancy Van Buren, and her cousin Jane Matthews came by my office at Digital Binary Components Corporation . . ."
    b. Good: "Martha and two other friends talked with me at work one day . . ."
    c. Good: "After living in five states and attending six universities, I finally graduated and got an engineering job."

DEVELOPING THE *BEFORE, HOW,* AND *AFTER* SECTIONS
Here are practical suggestions for developing the *before, how,* and *after* sections in your personal testimony.

1. **Before:**
    a. Many people's actions spring out of their unsatisfied deep inner needs. What were one or two of your unsatisfied deep inner needs before you came to know Jesus Christ? Some examples of inner needs are:

—lack of peace	—desire to be in control	—lack of significance
—fear of death	—loneliness	—no real friends
—something missing	—lack of security	—no motivation
—no meaning to life	—lack of purpose	

b. Non-Christians are usually trying to satisfy their deep inner needs through unsatisfactory solutions. In the past, what unsatisfactory solutions did you use to attempt to meet those deep inner needs? As you develop your testimony list positive as well as negative solutions you may have tried. Some examples are:

—marriage/family —sports/fitness —hobbies/entertainment
—work —money —sex
—drugs/alcohol —education —wrong friends

2. **How:**

a. Describe the circumstances that caused you to consider Christ as the solution to your deep inner needs. Identify the events that led to your conversion. In some cases this may have taken place over a period of time.

b. State specifically the steps you took to become a Christian. If there is a particular passage of Scripture that applies here, you may want to use it. Usually you will simply paraphrase it.

c. Include the gospel clearly and briefly. The gospel includes:

1) All have sinned.
2) Sin's penalty.
3) Christ paid the penalty.
4) Must receive Christ.

3. **After:**

a. State how Christ filled or is filling your deep inner needs. In the *before* you expressed your needs and how you tried unsuccessfully to meet them. You now want to briefly show the difference that Christ has made in your life.

b. Conclude with a statement like: "But the greatest benefit is that I know for certain that I have eternal life." The person you talk to will tend to comment on the last thing you say. Often it is natural to move from the testimony into a clear presentation of the gospel.

Choose Your Testimony Format—Samples/Worksheets

Read the three sample testimonies (pages 56-58). Then, come back and check the box beside the format which best fits your own story. As you write the first draft of your testimony, refer back to the sample testimony most like your own.

☐ FORMAT 1. ADULT CONVERSION
You trusted Christ as an adult. You have a distinct *before, how* and *after*.

☐ FORMAT 2. EARLY CONVERSION/ADULT FULL COMMITMENT
You need to evaluate whether the early conversion experience was genuine. If you conclude it was not genuine, then use Format 1 as your model. If it was genuine, your life has been characterized by spiritual immaturity, or a life-style similar to that of a non-Christian.

☐ FORMAT 3. EARLY CONVERSION/CONSISTENT GROWTH
You probably grew up with Christian parents and have a strong church background. You may have very little *before*.

SAMPLE TESTIMONY
FORMAT 1. ADULT CONVERSION

BEFORE

A few years ago I found myself lacking purpose in my life. Something was missing. Nothing seemed to fill the void.

I had majored in Electrical Engineering in college and got a great job when I graduated. I kept striving for one promotion after another, thinking that the next promotion would be the one that would satisfy me. But it never did. I began working longer and longer hours giving myself to my profession. This began to have a negative effect on my family. I kept telling my wife I was only doing it for her and the kids, but I knew otherwise. What started out as the "ideal" marriage was coming apart at the seams. It got to the point that I did not want to go home at night. "Happy hour" was more fun than arguments.

HOW

In my next job I was asked to attend an engineering seminar with David and Jack from work. David seemed to have a certain something that was missing in my life.

On the way home from the seminar David told me about how Christ had changed his life and had given him a whole new reason for living. Many of the things he said seemed to be directed right at me. He talked about having been successful in business but that he was always falling short of his goals and expectations. Then he said that the answer to his frustration was to have personally committed his life to Jesus Christ. He had admitted to God that he was living in disobedience and had turned control of his life over to God. He mentioned the Bible said that Christ had died on the cross so we could be forgiven for everything we had ever done wrong. I had heard this before, but now it seemed to make a lot more sense. A couple of days after I returned home I took a walk down by the lake near our house. I prayed and confessed to God some of the things I had done that I knew had hurt and displeased Him. I asked Christ to come into my life and take over, because I wasn't doing a very good job with it by myself.

AFTER

Well, there was no flash of light or earthquake, but I do know that I felt as if a large weight was lifted from my shoulders. Not everything is perfect now, but I do feel as if I have a whole new purpose for living. God has given me a whole new set of priorities to live by. But the greatest thing of all is that I know for certain that I have the gift of eternal life.

SAMPLE TESTIMONY
FORMAT 2. EARLY CONVERSION/ADULT DEEPER COMMITMENT

BEFORE FULL
COMMITMENT

Not too long ago you could have characterized my life as lacking any real inner peace. Everything around me seemed to be in utter turmoil. Nothing I did would ease the tension in my life.

It didn't seem as if anything could fill the longing that was growing in my heart. I thought I could fill that void by getting involved in activities. I joined the health spa, took tennis lessons, was involved in transporting our children to all their various activities. I considered going back to work part-time. Then my husband received a promotion and we were transferred to another city. If I had felt the pressure before, the move just added to the intensity. It seemed that the only relief I could gain was by taking tranquilizers, but that was only temporary and it scared me to realize that I was beginning to depend upon them for relief.

HOW

We had gotten out of the habit of attending church over the years, but the Johnsons invited us to go to church with them, so we started going. After we had attended for a couple of months, we decided to participate in a Bible study discussion group. There we met people who were fun but took their Christianity seriously. They began to challenge us to really commit our lives to Christ.

We reviewed some things I had heard while growing up: that we were all breaking God's laws and deserved to be separated from Him, but that God had provided the way to restore that relationship with Him. That provision was the death of His only Son, Jesus Christ. What I needed to do about it was acknowledge my disobedience to God and turn from it and ask Christ to come into my life as my Savior and Lord. So I asked Christ to take over my life.

AFTER

It wasn't until we got involved in that mid-week Bible study that I really understood what it meant to be committed to Jesus Christ. It was there that I learned that I could not gain inner peace in my life if I was going to try to run my own life. As a result of the Bible study I made a whole new commitment to Christ. The inner peace that I was striving for so desperately was finally there. But the greatest thing of all is that I know for certain that I have a personal relationship with God and have eternal life.

SAMPLE TESTIMONY
FORMAT 3: EARLY CONVERSION/CONSISTENT GROWTH

BEFORE

As I look around me I see people feverishly trying to fill voids in their lives. Men are giving themselves to their jobs, and in the process sacrificing their families. A number of my fellow workers seem to be trying to find meaning in their lives, but just when they think they have attained what they want, they realize these things are not meeting their deepest needs. I find myself being involved in many of these same activities, but I am finding satisfaction. What is the difference?

HOW

I realize that I'm not reacting to life the way many people do for a good reason. I have something in my life that has given me peace and purpose that many others do not have. I have discovered that a personal relationship with Jesus Christ fills the voids that many people are trying to fill with activities and things that just don't satisfy.

As I was growing up, my parents were very active in church. Because they were active, they figured that I should be also. So every Sunday, there we were. What was real to them was just a game to me. Then one summer I attended a church summer camp. This changed my whole view of "religion." I discovered at this camp that Christianity was more than a religion, it was a personal relationship with God through His Son, Jesus Christ. In the evenings our discussions centered around who Jesus Christ was and what He did. They were interesting to me. One day after we had finished sports my counselor asked me if I had ever personally committed my life to Jesus Christ or was I still thinking about it? I told him I was still thinking about it. We sat down and talked. He explained from the Bible what I would need to do in order to become a real Christian. I saw that I had done many things wrong and that the penalty was eternal death! I saw that Christ had died on the cross to set me free from that penalty. I prayed with my counselor right there and committed my life to Jesus Christ.

AFTER

As I grew physically I also grew spiritually. I find that when I try to do things my way and leave God out of the picture, I have the same struggles as everyone else. But when I let Him be in control, I experience a peace that can only come from Him. But the greatest thing of all is that I know for certain that I have eternal life.

TESTIMONY WORKSHEET
FORMAT 1. ADULT CONVERSION

Below is a list of questions for an Adult Conversion testimony. Jot down thoughts under each question. This will give you a basis from which to write sentences and paragraphs about your own experience as you prepare your first draft for Session 8.

BEFORE:

1. What was a deep inner need in your life before you met Christ?

2. Give some examples of how you tried to meet or fulfill that need with unsatisfactory solutions.

HOW:

1. Describe the circumstances that caused you to consider Christ.

2. State how you trusted Christ. (Briefly include the gospel).

AFTER:

1. Give an example of how Christ met or is currently meeting your deep inner needs.

2. End with a statement to the effect that you know for certain that you have eternal life.

After you have filled in the Testimony Worksheet and are ready to start writing you may find it difficult to know how to begin. The following examples may trigger some ideas for you:

- A few years ago I found myself lacking (deep inner need) in my life. (Develop the inner need.) I tried to meet that need by (develop the unsatisfactory solutions).
- A search for (deep inner need) would be the way you could have described my life not too long ago. (Develop the inner need.) I kept (develop the unsatisfactory solutions), but those things did not work.
- At one point in my life I was searching for (deep inner need), but nothing I did would satisfy that need. I tried (develop the unsatisfatory solutions).
- Not too long ago you could have characterized my life as/by (deep inner need). (Develop the inner need.) The things I tried did not help. (Develop the unsatisfactory solutions.)

TESTIMONY WORKSHEET
FORMAT 2: EARLY CONVERSION/ADULT DEEPER COMMITMENT

Below is a list of questions for an Early Conversion/Adult Deeper Commitment testimony. Jot down thoughts under each question. This will give you a basis from which to write sentences and paragraphs about your own experience as you prepare your first draft for Session 8.

BEFORE DEEPER COMMITMENT:

1. What was a deep inner need you were trying to fill?

2. Give some examples of how you tried to fill that inner need through unsatisfactory solutions.

HOW:

1. Briefly describe the situation in which you made a deeper commitment to Christ.

2. Refer back to your conversion experience. State how you trusted Christ. Briefly include the gospel.

AFTER:

1. State how Christ is currently meeting your deep inner needs.

2. End with a statement to the effect that you know for certain that you have eternal life.

After you have filled in the Testimony Worksheet and are ready to start writing, you may find it difficult to know how to begin. The following examples may trigger some ideas for you.

- A few years ago I found myself lacking (deep inner need) in my life. (Develop the inner need.) I tried to meet that need by (develop the unsatisfactory solutions).
- A search for (deep inner need) would be the way you could have described my life not too long ago. (Develop the inner need.) I kept (develop the unsatisfactory solutions), but those things did not work.
- At one point in my life I was searching for (deep inner need), but nothing I did would satisfy that need. I tried (develop the unsatisfactory solutions).
- Not too long ago you could have characterized my life as/by (deep inner need). (Develop the inner need.) The things I tried did not help. (Develop the unsatisfactory solutions.)

TESTIMONY WORKSHEET
FORMAT 3: EARLY CONVERSION/CONSISTENT GROWTH

Below is a list of questions for an Early Conversion/Consistent Growth testimony. Jot down thoughts under each question. This will give you a basis from which to write sentences and paragraphs about your own experience as you prepare your first draft for Session 8.

BEFORE:

1. State the deep inner needs you see people trying to fill.

2. Describe how you see people trying to satisfy those needs.

HOW:

1. Explain why you never experienced this problem.

2. Refer back to your conversion experience. State how you trusted Christ. Briefly include the gospel.

AFTER:

1. Illustrate how Christ met or is meeting your deep inner needs.

2. End with a statement to the effect that you know for certain that you have eternal life.

After you have filled in the Testimony Worksheet and are ready to start writing, you may find it difficult to know how to begin. The following examples may trigger some ideas for you.

- As I look around me I see people lacking (deep inner need) in their lives. (Develop the deep inner need.) They try to fill that void or those needs by (develop unsatisfactory solutions).
- I feel that many people are searching for (deep inner need). (Develop deep inner need.) They try many things to meet their need, such as (develop unsatisfactory solutions).

Workshop Outline For Session 8

1. You will read the first draft of your personal testimony and your leader will make suggestions for improvement.
2. Take notes from your leader's suggestions and rework your testimony.
3. Have your leader listen to your next draft. The leader will again make suggestions.
4. Repeat this procedure (points 3 and 4 above) until your testimony is completed.
5. When your written testimony is done, outline it on a 3"x5" card.
6. Practice giving your testimony from your 3"x5" card in four minutes or less to someone in your group.

ASSIGNMENT FOR SESSION 8:

1. Scripture Memory: Study and complete "Scripture Memory Instructions—Week Eight" (page 66). Memorize the second verse on "Fellowship," Hebrews 10:24-25.
2. Quiet Time: Continue reading, marking and recording.
3. Personal Testimony: Session eight is an extended class of three-to-four-hours. It is a workshop for intensive work on personal testimony preparation. Come rested and ready to work. Pray for God's wisdom for you, the other students and your leader. Write out a first draft of your testimony, using notes from your Testimony Worksheet. Be sure to bring this draft with you.
4. Other: Work on getting the requirements from Course 1 completed. Be ready to have several items initialed on your *Completion Record.*

Session 8

OUTLINE OF THIS SESSION:
1. Read the "Assignment for Session 9" (page 66).
2. Participate in the extended class session for refining your personal testimony.
3. Close in prayer.

Scripture Memory Instructions — Week Eight

About the Verse

TOPIC 5. FELLOWSHIP

We all need the mutual encouragement, admonition, and sharpening that Christian fellowship uniquely offers. The first-century believers saw this fellowship as essential: "They devoted themselves to the apostles' teaching and to the fellowship, to the breaking of bread and to prayer" (Acts 2:42).

Hebrews 10:24-25 — This verse teaches that we should encourage one another to love and good works through regular fellowship. Our faith and obedience to Christ can be stimulated by fellowship with other believers, as can theirs by fellowship with us.

Your Weekly Plan

1. Place 1 John 1:3 inside your pack with the other verses to be reviewed, and keep Hebrews 10:24-25 showing in the window.

2. Your goal should be to repeat each verse in your pack once a day. However, the more time you invest in your verses the more you will profit.

3. Check your new verse by writing it out or quoting it to someone by the end of the week.

ASSIGNMENT FOR SESSION 9:
1. Scripture Memory: Study and complete "Scripture Memory Instructions — Week Nine" (page 67). Memorize the verses on "Witnessing," Matthew 4:19 and Romans 1:16.
2. Quiet Time: Continue reading, marking, and recording.
3. Personal Testimony:
   a. Practice presenting your testimony using a 3"x5" card outline.
   b. Read the material on the *Lead-in* and *Close* to the personal testimony (pages 67-68).
4. Other:
   a. Work on getting everything you can completed and ready to be signed on your *Completion Record*.
   b. Carefully read and mark *My Heart Christ's Home* (pages 69-73) and complete "A Discussion of *My Heart Christ's Home*" (pages 74-75).

Session 9

OUTLINE OF THIS SESSION:

1. Break into review groups and quote the verses on "Witnessing," Matthew 4:19 and Romans 1:16. (Work at getting everything signed that you can on your *Completion Record.*)
2. Take the opportunity to give completed testimonies from a 3"x5" card outline.
3. Discuss the *Lead-in* and *Close* to the personal testimony (pages 67-68).
4. Discuss *My Heart Christ's Home* (pages 69-75).
5. Read the "Assignment for Session 10" (page 76).
6. Close in prayer: Focus on highlights from *My Heart Christ's Home.*

Scripture Memory Instructions — Week Nine

About the Verses

TOPIC 6. WITNESSING

God has given Christians the privilege and responsibility of reaching those who are without Christ. We are on earth to be His witnesses.

Matthew 4:19 — Jesus challenged two fishermen with the infinitely greater value of fishing for men. Whatever our occupation, Jesus wants us to follow Him and be involved with Him in reaching others with the Gospel.

Romans 1:16 — We should unashamedly share the Gospel, God's power to save, which is the only real answer to the needs of men and women. Jesus said, "Whoever acknowledges me before men, I will also acknowledge him before my Father in heaven" (Matthew 10:32).

The phrase, "first for the Jew, then for the Gentile," means that the gospel is for all people (Romans 1:16) and has universal meaning.

Your Weekly Plan

1. Place Matthew 4:19 and Romans 1:16 in the window of your pack. You will learn these two verses this week.

2. By the end of the week, write out these verses or quote them to someone before coming to class.

Lead-in to Personal Testimony

You have just learned how to give your personal testimony in an organized manner. Questions may come to mind. "When do I share it?" "How do I direct the conversation so it will lead to presenting my testimony?" You may find the following suggestions helpful.

1. Include some "small talk" before discussing spiritual matters. Discuss family, job, hobbies, interests, etc.
2. Be alert for needs expressed. They may be talking about family problems or stress on the job. You can use these to show how Christ has helped you through some of the same areas.
3. Discuss past concerns and needs that you had in your life. "We used to struggle in our marriage relationship," or, "I used to allow the pressures at work to get to me." "Then I discovered something that made a tremendous difference in my life."
4. Discuss contemporary situations that are happening in the news or in your area. "I saw on TV that drugs are epidemic in our country. It seems that people are trying to find something that satisfies so they are turning to drugs. These same people are saying it does not work."
5. Build relationships with them. It may take 10 minutes or 10 hours or 10 days or 10 months—but build relationships.
6. Don't condemn them for living like non-Christians, they are non-Christians. Your objective is to share how they can have a better life in Christ.
7. Avoid dogmatic "religious" statements. "Jesus is the answer to all your problems." He is, but they don't even know *who* He is, much less what He can *do* in their lives.
8. Avoid arguments on moral issues. You can expect non-Christians to have conflicts with clear biblical teaching. Remember they do not have a valid base to make correct moral decisions.

The Close

When you have shared your personal testimony, you may want to conclude with a statement that causes the person to reflect on what you have just shared. What you say will depend on how this person has been responding to what you have shared. If their response seems positive you could say something like:

1. "Bill, has anything like this ever happened to you?"
2. "Mary, do you know for certain whether you have eternal life?"
3. "Do you have any idea what eternal life is?"
4. "May I share with you some day how I know for certain that I have eternal life?"
5. "May I share an illustration with you that explains how a person can know for certain that he has eternal life?"

If their response seems negative or neutral you could say something like:

1. "If you are interested I would like to share more with you sometime."
2. "Do you have any questions on what I have just shared with you?"
3. "Well, that is what happened to me. If you ever want to talk about it any further, I would love to do so."

Keep in mind that the personal testimony is not a convincing tool. The testimony is the "bait" and the gospel is the "hook."

My Heart Christ's Home

Robert Boyd Munger

In Paul's epistle to the Ephesians, we find these words: "That [God] would grant you, according to the riches of His glory, to be strengthened with might by His Spirit in the inner man; that Christ may dwell in your hearts by faith" (Ephesians 3:16). Or, as another has translated, "That Christ may settle down and be at home in your hearts by faith."

Without question one of the most remarkable Christian doctrines is that Jesus Christ Himself through the presence of the Holy Spirit will actually enter a heart, settle down and be at home there. Christ will make the human heart His abode.

Our Lord said to His disciples, "If a man love Me, he will keep My words: and My Father will love him, and We will come unto him, and make Our abode with him" (John 14:23). It was difficult for them to understand what He was saying. How was it possible for Him to make His abode with them in this sense?

It is interesting that our Lord used the same word here that He gave them in the first part of the fourteenth chapter of John: "I go to prepare a place for you . . . that where I am, ye may be also." Our Lord was promising His disciples that, just as He was going to heaven to prepare a place for them and would welcome them one day, now it would be possible for them to prepare a place for Him in their hearts and He would come and make His abode with them.

They could not understand this. How could it be?

Then came Pentecost. The Spirit of the living Christ was given to the church and they understood. God did not dwell in Herod's temple in Jerusalem! God did not dwell in a temple made with hands; but now, through the miracle of the outpoured Spirit, God would dwell in human hearts. The body of the believer would be the temple of the living God and the human heart would be the home of Jesus Christ.

It is difficult for me to think of a higher privilege than to make for Christ a home in my heart, to welcome, to serve, to please, to fellowship with Him there. One evening that I shall never forget, I invited Him into my heart. What an entrance He made! It was not a spectacular, emotional thing, but very real. It was at the very center of my life. He came into the darkness of my heart and turned on the light. He built a fire in the cold hearth and banished the chill. He started music where there had been stillness and He filled the emptiness with His own loving, wonderful fellowship. I have never regretted opening the door to Christ and I never will—not into eternity!

This, of course, is the first step in making the heart Christ's home. He has said, "Behold, I stand at the door and knock: if any man hear My voice, and open the door, I will come in to him, and will sup with him, and he with Me" (Revelation 3:20). If you are interested in making your life an abode of the living God, let me encourage you to invite Christ into your heart and He will surely come.

After Christ entered my heart and in the joy of that new-found relationship, I said to Him, "Lord, I want this heart of mine to be Yours. I want to have You settle down here and be perfectly at home. Everything I have belongs to You. Let me show You around and introduce You to the various features of the home that You may be more comfortable and that we may have fuller fellowship together." He was very glad to come, of course, and happier still to be given a place in the heart.

The Library

The first room was the study—the library. Let us call it the study of the mind. Now in my home this room of the mind is a very small room with very thick walls. But it is an important room. In a sense, it is the control room of the house. He entered with me and looked around at the books in the bookcase, the magazines upon the table, the pictures on the wall. As I followed His gaze, I became uncomfortable. Strangely enough, I had not felt badly about this before, but now that He was there looking at these things I was embarrassed. There were some books there that His eyes were too pure to behold. There was a lot of trash and literature on the table that a Christian had no business reading and as for the pictures on the wall—the imaginations and thoughts of my mind— these were shameful.

I turned to Him and said, "Master, I know that this room needs a radical alteration. Will You help me make it what it ought to be—to bring every thought into captivity to You?"

"Surely," He said. "Gladly will I help you. That is one reason I am here. First of all, take all the things that you are reading and seeing which are not helpful, pure, good and true, and throw them out! Now put on the empty shelves the books of the Bible. Fill the library with Scriptures and meditate on them day and night. As for the pictures on the wall, you will have difficulty controlling these images, but here is an aid." He gave me a full-sized portrait of Himself. "Hang this centrally," He said, "on the wall of the mind." I did and I have discovered through the years that when my thoughts are centered upon Christ Himself, His purity and power cause impure imaginations to retreat. So He has helped me to bring my thoughts into captivity.

May I suggest to you if you have difficulty with this little room of the mind, that you bring Christ in there. Pack it full with the Word of God, meditate upon it and keep before it ever the immediate presence of the Lord Jesus.

The Dining Room
From the study we went into the dining room, the room of appetites and desires. Now this was a very large room. I spent a good deal of time in the dining room and much effort in satisfying my wants.

I said to him, "This is a very commodious room and I am quite sure You will be pleased with what we serve here."

He seated Himself at the table with me and asked, "What is on the menu for dinner?"

"Well," I said, "my favorite dishes: old bones, corn husks, sour cabbage, leeks, onions and garlic right out of Egypt." These were the things I liked—worldly fare. I suppose there was nothing radically wrong in any particular item, but it was not the food that should satisfy the life of a real Christian. When the food was placed before Him, He said nothing about it. However, I observed that He did not eat it, and I said to Him, somewhat disturbed, "Savior, You don't care for the food that is placed before You? What is the trouble?"

He answered, "I have meat to eat that ye know not of. My meat is to do the will of Him that sent Me." He looked at me again and said, "If you want food that really satisfies you, seek the will of the Father, not your own pleasures, not your own desires, not your own satisfaction. Seek to please Me, and that food will satisfy you." And there about the table He gave me a taste of doing God's will. What a flavor! There is no food like it in all the world. It alone satisfies. Everything else is dissatisfying in the end.

Now if Christ is in your heart, and I trust He is, what kind of food are you serving Him and what kind of food are you eating yourself? Are you living for the lust of the flesh and the pride of life—selfishly? Or are you choosing God's will for your meat and drink?

The Drawing Room
We walked next into the drawing room. This room was rather intimate and comfortable. I liked it. It had a fireplace, overstuffed chairs, a bookcase, sofa, and a quiet atmosphere.

He also seemed pleased with it. He said, "This is indeed a delightful room. Let us come here often. It is secluded and quiet and we can have fellowship together."

Well, naturally, as a young Christian I was thrilled. I could not think of anything I would rather do than have a few minutes apart with Christ in intimate comradeship.

He promised, "I will be here every morning early. Meet with Me here and we will start the day together." So, morning after morning, I would come downstairs to the drawing room and He would take a book of the Bible from the bookcase. He would open it and then we would read together. He would tell me of its riches and unfold to me its truths. He would make my heart warm as He revealed His love and His grace toward me. They were wonderful hours together. In fact, we called the drawing room the "withdrawing room." It was a period when we had our quiet time together.

But little by little, under the pressure of many responsibilities, this time began to be shortened. Why, I don't know, but I thought I was just too busy to spend time with Christ. This was not intentional, you understand; it just happened that way. Finally, not only was the time shortened, but I began to miss a day now and then. It was examinations time at the university. Then it was some other urgent emergency. I would miss it two days in a row and often more.

I remember one morning when I was in a hurry, rushing down the steps, eager to be on my way.

As I passed the drawing room, the door was ajar. Looking in I saw a fire in the fireplace and the Lord sitting there. Suddenly in dismay, I thought to myself, "He was my guest. I had invited Him into my heart! He had come as Lord of my home. And yet here I am neglecting Him." I turned and went in. With downcast glance I said, "Blessed Master, forgive me. Have You been here all these mornings?"

"Yes," He said, "I told you I would be here every morning to meet with you." Then I was even more ashamed. He had been faithful in spite of my faithlessness. I asked His forgiveness and He readily forgave me, as He does when we are truly penitent.

He said, "The trouble with you is this: You have been thinking of the quiet time, of the Bible study and prayer time, as a factor in your own spiritual progress, but you have forgotten that this hour means something to Me also. Remember, I love you.

I have redeemed you at a great cost. I desire your fellowship. Now," He said, "do not neglect this hour if only for My sake. Whatever else may be your desire, remember I want your fellowship!"

You know, the truth that Christ wants my fellowship, that He loves me, wants me to be with Him, wants to be with me and waits for me, has done more to transform my quiet time with God than any other single fact. Don't let Christ wait alone in the drawing room of your heart, but every day find some time when, with the Word of God and in prayer, you may fellowship with Him.

The Workshop
Before long He asked, "Do you have a workshop in your home?" Down in the basement of the home of my heart I had a workbench and some equipment, but I was not doing much with it. Once in a while I would go down and fuss around with a few little gadgets, but I wasn't producing anything substantial or worthwhile.

I led Him down there.

He looked over the workbench and what little talents and skills I had. He said, "This is quite well furnished. What are you producing with your life for the Kingdom of God?" He looked at one or two of the little toys that I had thrown together on the bench and He held one up to me. "Are these little toys all that you are producing in your Christian life?"

"Well," I said, "Lord, that is the best I can do. I know it isn't much and I really want to do more, but after all, I have no skill or strength."

"Would you like to do better?" He asked.

"Certainly," I replied.

"All right. Let Me have your hands. Now relax in Me and let My Spirit work through you. I know you are unskilled and clumsy and awkward, but the Spirit is the Master-worker and if He controls your hands and your heart He will work through you." And so, stepping around behind me and putting His great strong hands over mine, controlling the tools with His skillful fingers, He began to work through me.

There's much more that I must still learn

and I am very far from satisfied with the product that is being turned out, but I do know that whatever has been produced for God has been through His strong hand and through the power of His Spirit in me.

Do not become discouraged because you cannot do much for God. Your ability is not the fundamental condition. It is He who is controlling your fingers and upon whom you are relying. Give your talents and gifts to God and He will do things with them that will surprise you.

The Rumpus Room

I remember the time He inquired about the playroom. I was hoping He would not ask me about that. There were certain associations and friendships, activities and amusements that I wanted to keep for myself. I did not think Christ would enjoy them or approve of them, so I evaded the question.

But there came an evening when I was leaving to join some companions—I was in college at the time—and as I was about to cross the threshold, He stopped me with a glance. "Are you going out?"

I answered, "Yes."

"Good," He said, "I would like to go with you."

"Oh," I replied rather awkwardly. "I don't think, Lord, that You would really want to go with us. Let's go out tomorrow night. Tomorrow night we will go to prayer meeting, but tonight I have another appointment."

He said, "That's all right. Only I thought when I came into your home we were going to do everything together. We were going to be partners. I want you to know that I am willing to go with you."

"Well," I said, "we will go some place together tomorrow night."

But that evening I spent some miserable hours. I felt wretched. What kind of a friend was I to Christ, when I was deliberately leaving Him out of my associations, doing things and going places that I knew very well He would not enjoy? When I returned that evening, there was a light in His room and I went up to talk it over with Him. I said, "Lord, I have learned my lesson.

I cannot have a good time without You. We will do everything together from now on."

Then we went down into the rumpus room of the house and He transformed it. He brought into life real joy, real happiness, real satisfaction, real friendship. Laughter and music have been ringing in the house ever since.

The Hall Closet

There is just one more matter that I might share with you. One day I found Him waiting for me at the door. There was an arresting look in His eye. He said to me as I entered, "There is a peculiar odor in the house. There is something dead around here. It's upstairs. I think it is in the hall closet." As soon as He said the words, I knew what He was talking about. Yes, there was a small hall closet up there on the landing, just a few feet square, and in that closet behind lock and key I had one or two little personal things that I did not want Christ to see. I knew they were dead and rotting things. And yet I loved them, and I wanted them so for myself that I was afraid to admit that they were there. I went up the stairs with Him and as we mounted, the odor became stronger and stronger. He pointed at the door and said, "It's in there! Some dead thing!"

I was angry. That's the only way I can put it. I had given Him access to the library, the dining room, the drawing room, the work shop, the rumpus room, and now He was asking me about a little two-by-four closet. I said inwardly, "This is too much. I am not going to give Him the key."

"Well," He said, reading my thoughts, "If you think I am going to stay up here on the second floor with this odor, you are mistaken. I will take My bed out on the back porch. I'm certainly not going to put up with that." And I saw Him start down the stairs.

When you have come to know and love Christ, the worst thing that can happen is to sense His fellowship retreating from you. I had to surrender. "I'll give you the key," I said sadly, "but You'll have to open the closet. You'll have to clean it out. I haven't the strength to do it."

"I know," He said, "I know you haven't. Just give Me the key. Just authorize Me to take care of that closet and I will." So, with trembling fingers I passed the key over to Him. He took it from my hand, walked over to the door, opened it, entered it, took out all the putrefying stuff that was rotting there and threw it away. Then He cleansed the closet, painted it, fixed it up, doing it all in a moment's time. Oh, what victory and release to have that dead thing out of my life!

Transferring the Title

Then a thought came to me. I said to myself, "I have been trying to keep this heart of mine clear for Christ. I start on one room and no sooner have I cleaned that than another room is dirty. I begin on the second room and the first room becomes dusty again. I am so tired and weary trying to maintain a clean heart and an obedient life. I just am not up to it!" So I ventured a question: "Lord, is there any chance that You would take over the responsibility of the whole house and operate it for me and with me just as You did that closet? Would you take the responsibility to keep my heart what it ought to be and my life where it ought to be?"

I could see His face light up as He replied, "Certainly, that is what I came to do. You cannot be a victorious Christian in your own strength. That is impossible. Let Me do it through you and for you. That is the way. But," He added slowly, "I am not owner of this house. I am just a guest. I have no authority to proceed since the property is not Mine."

I saw it in a minute and dropping to my knees, I said, "Lord, You have been a guest, and I have been the host. From now on I am going to be the servant. You are going to be the Lord." Running as fast as I could to the strong box, I took out the title deed to the house describing its assets and liabilities, its situation and condition. Then returning to Him, I eagerly signed it over to belong to Him alone for time and eternity. "Here it is, all that I am and have forever. Now You run the house. I'll just remain with You as houseboy and friend."

He took my life that day and I can give you my word, there is no better way to live the Christian life. He knows how to keep it in shape and deep peace settles down on the soul. May Christ settle down and be at home in your heart as Lord of all.

I am the Lord's! O joy beyond expression,
　O sweet response to voice of love Divine;
Faith's joyous "Yes" to the assuring whisper,
　"Fear not! I have redeemed thee;
　　thou art Mine."

I am the Lord's! It is the glad confession
　Wherewith the Bride recalls the happy day,
When love's "I will" accepted Him forever,
　"The Lord's," to love, to honor and obey.

I am the Lord's! Yet teach me all it meaneth,
　All it involves of love and loyalty,
Of holy service, absolute surrender,
　And unreserved obedience unto Thee.

I am the Lord's! Yes; body, soul and spirit,
　O seal them irrecoverably Thine:
As Thou, Beloved, in Thy grace and fullness
　Forever and forever more art mine.

　　　　by Lucy A. Bennett
　　　　from Hymns (InterVarsity Press)

©1954 by Inter-Varsity Christian Fellowship. Reprinted by permission of InterVarsity Press, Downers Grove, Illinois 60515.

A Discussion of My Heart Christ's Home

Certainly acknowledging Jesus Christ as Lord is a major step of commitment and surrender that every Christian at some point must face. Two verses that imply this important issue are:

"Choose for yourselves this day whom you will serve."

—Joshua 24:15

"Therefore, I urge you, brothers, in view of God's mercy, to offer your bodies as living sacrifices, holy and pleasing to God—this is your spiritual act of worship."

—Romans 12:1

It is also true that Christ, as we allow Him, will increasingly take over our lives and gradually come to completely control them. This is the theme of *My Heart Christ's Home*. The following verses emphasize that concept:

"I don't mean to say I am perfect. I haven't learned all I should even yet, but I keep working toward that day when I will finally be all that Christ saved me for and wants me to be."

—Philippians 3:12 LB

"But we all, with unveiled face beholding as in a mirror the glory of the Lord, are being transformed into the same image from glory to glory, just as from the Lord, the Spirit."

—2 Corinthians 3:18 NASB

"But be constantly growing in the sphere of grace and an experiential knowledge of our Lord and Savior Jesus Christ. To Him be glory both now and to the day of eternity."

—2 Peter 3:18 Wuest

"So let us know, let us press on to know the Lord. His going forth is as certain as the dawn; and He will come to us like the rain, like the spring rain watering the earth."

—Hosea 6:3 NASB

Under the following seven headings, write down several words or phrases that describe what the author was referring to in each analogy in *My Heart Christ's Home*.

THE LIBRARY

_____

_____

_____

_____

_____

THE DINING ROOM

_____
_____
_____
_____

THE DRAWING ROOM

_____
_____
_____
_____

THE WORKSHOP

_____
_____
_____
_____

THE RUMPUS ROOM (Recreation Room)

_____
_____
_____
_____

THE HALL CLOSET

_____
_____
_____
_____

TRANSFERRING THE TITLE

_____
_____
_____
_____

ASSIGNMENT FOR SESSION 10:

1. Scripture Memory: Diligently polish up all the verses you know.
2. Quiet Time: Continue reading, marking, recording and using your Evangelism Prayer List.
3. Personal Testimony: Come prepared to give your testimony to the class from the outline on your 3"x5" card.
4. Other:
   a. Study and mark *How to Spend a Day in Prayer* (pages 77-82). Give careful thought to how you will apply these principles in Session 11.
   b. Be sure to have everything signed that you can on your *Completion Record* at the next class session.

Session 10

OUTLINE OF THIS SESSION:

1. Break into verse review groups and quote all the verses you have learned in Course 1.
2. Share some quiet time thoughts, primarily from your *Highlights Record*.
3. Take the opportunity to give testimonies from a 3" x 5" card outline.
4. Briefly share results from using your Prayer Sheets.
5. Confirm the time and place for Session 11—your half day in prayer.
6. Discuss *How to Spend a Day in Prayer* (pages 77-82), the section "Why a Day in Prayer?" (page 83), and "Divide the Day into Three Parts" (page 84).
7. Discuss "How to Stay Awake and Alert" and "How to Make a Worry List" (pages 84-85).
8. Discuss "A Checklist for a Day in Prayer" (page 85).
9. Discuss "How to Take Notes During a Half Day in Prayer" (page 86).
10. Read the "Assignment for Session 11" (page 87).
11. Close in prayer. Focus on people on your Evangelism Prayer Lists and any upcoming "relating activity."

How to Spend a Day in Prayer
Lorne C. Sanny

"Prayer is a powerful thing, for God has bound and tied Himself thereto."
— Martin Luther

"Avail yourself of the greatest privilege this side of heaven. Jesus Christ died to make this communion and communication with the Father possible."
— Billy Graham

"God acquaintance is not made hurriedly. He does not bestow His gifts on the casual or hasty comer and goer. To be much alone with God is the secret of knowing Him and of influence with Him."
— E.M. Bounds

"I never thought a day could make such a difference," a friend said to me. "My relationship to everyone seems improved."

"Why don't I do it more often?"

Comments like these come from those who set aside a personal day of prayer.

With so many activities—important ones—clamoring for our time, real prayer is considered more a luxury than a necessity. How much more so spending a *day* in prayer!

The Bible gives us three time-guides for personal prayer. There is the command to "pray without ceasing"—the spirit of prayer—keeping so in tune with God that we can lift our hearts in request or praise anytime through the day.

There is also the practice of a quiet time or morning watch—seen in the life of David (Psalm 5:3), of Daniel (6:10), and of

77

the Lord Jesus (Mark 1:35). This daily time specified for meditation in the Word of God and prayer is indispensable to the growing, healthy Christian.

Then there are examples in the Scripture of extended time given to prayer alone. Jesus spent whole nights praying. Nehemiah prayed "certain days" upon hearing of the plight of Jerusalem. Three times Moses spent 40 days and 40 nights alone with God.

Learning from God
I believe it was in these special times of prayer that God made known His ways and His plans to Moses (Psalm 103:7). He allowed Moses to look through a chink in the fence and gain special insights, while the rank-and-file Israelites saw only the *acts* of God as they unfolded day by day.

Once I remarked to Dawson Trotman, founder of The Navigators, "You impress me as one who feels he is a man of destiny, one destined to be used of God."

"I don't think that's the case," he replied, "but I know this. God *has* given me some promises that I know He will fulfill." During earlier years Daws spent countless protracted times alone with God, and out of these times the Navigator work grew—not by methods or principles, but by promises given to him from the Word.

In my own life one of the most refreshing and stabilizing factors, as well as the means for new direction or confirmation of the will of God, has been those extended times of prayer—in the neighborhood park in Seattle, on a hill behind the Navigator home in Southern California, or out in the Garden of the Gods here in Colorado Springs.

These special prayer times can become anchor points in your life, times when you "drive a stake" as a landmark and go on from there. Your daily quiet time is more effective as you pray into day-by-day reality some of the things the Lord speaks to your heart in protracted times of prayer. The quiet time in turn is the foundation for "praying without ceasing," going through the day in communion with God.

Perhaps you haven't spent a protracted time in prayer because you haven't recog-nized the need for it. Or maybe you aren't sure what you would do with a whole day on your hands *just to pray.*

Why a Day of Prayer?
Why take this time from a busy life? What is it for?

1. *For extended fellowship with God*—beyond your morning devotions. It means just plain being with and thinking about God. God has called us into the fellowship of His Son, Jesus Christ (1 Corinthians 1:9). Like many personal relationships, this fellowship is nurtured by spending time together. God takes special note of times when His people reverence Him and *think upon His Name* (Malachi 3:16).

2. *For a renewed perspective.* Like flying over the battlefield in a reconnaissance plane, a day of prayer gives opportunity to think of the world from God's point of view. Especially when going through some difficulty we need this perspective to sharpen our vision of the unseen, and to let the immediate, tangible things drop into proper place. Our spiritual defenses are strengthened while "we fix our eyes not on what is seen, but on what is unseen. For . . . what is unseen is eternal" (2 Corinthians 4:18).

3. *For catching up on intercession.* There are non-Christian friends and relatives to bring before the Lord, missionaries on various fields, our pastors, our neighbors and Christian associates, our government leaders—to name a few. Influencing people and changing events through prayer is well known among Christians but too little prac-ticed. And as times become more serious around us, we need to reconsider the value of personal prayer, both to accomplish and to deter.

4. *For prayerful consideration of our own lives before the Lord*—personal inventory and evaluation. You will especially want to take a day of prayer when facing important decisions, as well as on a periodic basis. On such a day you can evaluate where you are in relation to your goals, and get direction from the Lord through His Word. Promises are there for you and me, just as they have been for Hudson Taylor or George Mueller.

or Dawson Trotman. And it is in our times alone with God that He gives inner assurance of His promises to us.

5. *For adequate preparation.* Nehemiah, after spending "certain days" seeking the Lord in prayer, was called in before the king. "Then the king said unto me, 'For what dost thou make request?' So I prayed to the God of heaven. And I said unto the king, 'If it please the king . . .'"—and he outlined his plan (Nehemiah 2:4-5, KJV). Then Nehemiah says, "I arose in the night, I and some few men with me; neither told I any man what my God had put in my heart to do at Jerusalem" (2:12). When did God put in his heart this plan? I believe it was when he fasted and prayed and waited on God. Then when the day came for action, he was ready.

I heard a boy ask a pilot if it didn't take quick thinking to land his plane when something went wrong. The pilot answered that no, he knew at all times where he would put down *if* something went wrong. He had that thought out ahead of time.

So it should be in our Christian life. If God has given us plans and purposes in those times alone, we will be ready when opportunity comes to move right into it. We won't have to say, "I'm not prepared." The reason many Christians are dead to opportunities is not because they are not mentally alert, but they are simply unprepared in heart. Preparation is made when we get alone with God.

Pray on the Basis of God's Word
Daniel said, "In the first year of his reign (the reign of Darius), I, Daniel, understood from the Scriptures, according to the word of the Lord given to Jeremiah the prophet, that the desolation of Jerusalem would last seventy years. So I turned to the Lord God and pleaded with Him in prayer and petition, in fasting, and in sackcloth and ashes. I prayed to the Lord my God and confessed" (Daniel 9:2-4).

He understood by the Scriptures what was to come. And as a result of his exposure to the Word of God, he prayed. It has been said that God purposes, therefore He promises. And we can add, "Therefore I pray the promises, so that God's purposes might come to reality." God purposed to do something, and He promised it, therefore Daniel prayed. This was Daniel's part in completing the circuit, like an electrical circuit, so that the power could flow through.

Your day alone with the Lord isn't a matter of sitting out on a rock like the statue of *The Thinker* and taking whatever thoughts come to your mind. That's not safe. It should be a day exposed to God's Word, and then His Word leads you into prayer. You will end the day worse than you started if all you do is engage in introspection, thinking of yourself and your own problems. It isn't your estimate of yourself that counts anyway. It's God's estimate. And He will reveal His estimate to you by the Holy Spirit through His Word, the open Bible. And then the Word leads into prayer.

How to go About It
How do you go about it? Having set aside a day or portion of a day for prayer, pack a lunch and start out. Find a place where you can be alone, away from distractions. This may be a wooded area near home, or your backyard. An outdoor spot is excellent if you can find it; but don't get sidetracked into nature studies and fritter away your time. If you find yourself watching the squirrels or the ants, direct your observation by reading Psalm 104 and meditating on the power of God in creation.

Take along a Bible, a notebook and pencil, a hymnbook, and perhaps a devotional book. I like to have with me the booklet *Power Through Prayer* by E.M. Bounds and read a chapter or two as a challenge to the strategic value of prayer. Or I sometimes take Horatius Bonar's *Words to Winners of Souls,* or a missionary biography like *Behind the Ranges* by Mary C. Taylor, which records the prayer victories of J. O. Fraser in inland China.

Even if you have all day, you will want to use it profitably. So lose no time in starting, and start purposefully.

Wait on the Lord

Divide the day into three parts: waiting on the Lord, prayer for others, and prayer for yourself.

As you *wait on the Lord,* don't hurry. You will miss the point if you look for some mystical or ecstatic experience. Just seek the Lord, waiting on *Him.* Isaiah 40:31 promises that those who wait upon the Lord will renew their strength. Psalm 27:14 is one of dozens of verses which mention waiting on Him. Psalm 62:5 says, "My soul, wait thou only upon God; for my expectation is from Him."

Wait on Him first to *realize His presence.* Read through a passage like Psalm 139, grasping the truth of His presence with you as you read each verse. Ponder the impossibility of being anywhere in the universe where He is not. Often we are like Jacob when he said, "Surely the Lord is in this place; and I knew it not" (Genesis 28:16, KJV).

Wait on Him also *for cleansing.* The last two verses of Psalm 139 lead you into this. Ask God to search your heart as these verses suggest. When we search our own hearts it can lead to imaginations, morbid introspection, or anything the enemy may want to throw before us. But when the Holy Spirit searches He will bring to your attention that which should be confessed and cleansed. Psalms 51 and 32, David's songs of confession, will help you. Stand upon the firm ground of 1 John 1:9 and claim God's faithfulness to forgive whatever specific thing you confess.

If you realize you've sinned against a brother, make a note of it so you won't forget to set it right. Otherwise, the rest of the day will be hindered. God won't be speaking to you if there is something between you and someone else that you haven't planned to take care of at the earliest possible moment.

As you wait on God, ask for the power of concentration. Bring yourself back from daydreaming.

Next, wait on God *to worship Him.* Psalms 103, 111, and 145 are wonderful portions to follow as you praise the Lord for the greatness of His power. Most of the psalms are prayers. Or turn to Revelation, chapters 4 and 5, and use them in your praise to Him. There is no better way to pray scripturally than to pray Scripture.

If you brought a hymnbook you can sing to the Lord. Some wonderful hymns have been written that put into words what we could scarcely express ourselves. Maybe you don't sing very well—then be sure you're out of earshot of someone else and "make a joyful noise unto the Lord." *He* will appreciate it.

This will lead you naturally into thanksgiving. Reflect upon the wonderful things God has done for you and thank Him for these—for your own salvation and spiritual blessings, for your family, friends, and opportunities. Go beyond that which you thank the Lord for daily and take time to express appreciation to Him for countless things He's given.

Prayer for Others

Now is the time for the unhurried, more detailed prayer for others that you don't get to ordinarily. Remember people in addition to those for whom you usually pray. Trace your way around the world, praying for people by countries.

Here are three suggestions as to what to pray:

First, ask specific things for them. Perhaps you remember or have jotted down various needs people have mentioned. Use requests from missionary prayer letters. Pray for spiritual strength, courage, physical stamina, mental alertness, and so on. Imagine yourself in the situations where these people are and pray accordingly.

Second, look up some of the prayers in Scripture. Pray what Paul prayed for other people in the first chapter of Philippians and Colossians, and in the first and third chapters of Ephesians. This will help you advance in your prayer from the stage of "Lord, bless so and so and help them to do such and such."

Third, ask for others what you are praying for yourself. Desire for them what the Lord has shown *you.*

If you pray a certain verse or promise of

Scripture for a person you may want to put the reference by his name on your prayer list, and use this verse as you pray for that person the next time. Then use it for thanksgiving as you see the Lord answer.

Prayer for Yourself

The third part of your day will be prayer for yourself. If you are facing an important decision you may want to put this before prayer for others.

Again, let your prayer be ordered by Scripture and ask the Lord for understanding according to Psalm 119:18. Meditate upon verses of Scripture you have memorized or promises you have previously claimed from the Word. Reading a whole book of the Bible through, perhaps aloud, is a good idea. Consider how it might apply to your life.

In prayer for yourself, 1 Chronicles 4:10 is one good example to follow. Jabez prayed, "Oh that You would bless me and enlarge my territory! Let Your hand be with me, and keep me from harm so that I will be free from pain." That's prayer for your personal life, for your growth, for God's presence, and for God's protection. Jabez prayed in the will of God and God granted his request.

"Lord, what do *You* think of my life?" is the attitude of this portion of your day of prayer. Consider your main objctives in the light of what you know to be God's will for you. Jesus said, "My food is to do the will of Him who sent Me and to finish His work" (John 4:34). Do you want to do God's will more than anything else?

Then consider your activities—what you *do*—in the context of your objectives. God may speak to you about rearranging your schedule, cutting out certain activities that are good but not best, or some things that are entanglements or impediments to progress. Strip them off. You may be convicted about how you spend your evenings or Saturdays, when you could use the time to advantage and still get the recreation you need.

As you pray, record your thoughts on your activities and use of time, and plan for better scheduling. Perhaps the need for better preparation for your Sunday school class or a personal visit with an individual will come to your mind. Or the Lord may impress you to do something special for someone. Make a note of it.

During this part of your day, bring up any problems or decisions you are facing and seek the mind of God on them. It helps to list the factors involved in these decisions or problems. Pray over these factors and look into the Scriptures for guidance. You may be led to a promise or direction from the passages with which you have already filled your mind during the day.

After prayer, you may reach some definite conclusions upon which you can base firm convictions. It should be your aim in a day of prayer to come away with some conclusions and specific direction—some stakes driven. However, do not be discouraged if this is not the case. It may not be God's time for a conclusive answer to your problem. And you may discover that your real need was not to know the next step but to have a new revelation of God Himself.

In looking for promises to claim there's no need to thumb through looking for new or startling ones. Just start with the promises you already know. If you have been through the *Topical Memory System,* start by meditating on the verses in the *Rely on God's Resources* section. Chew over some old familiar promises the Lord has given you before, ones you remember as you think back. Pray about applying these verses to your life.

I have found some of the greatest blessings from a new realization of promises I already knew. And the familiar promises may lead you to others. The Bible is full of them.

You may want to mark or underline in your Bible the promises the Lord gives during these protracted times alone, and put the date and a word or two in the margin beside them.

Variety is important during your day of prayer. Read a while, pray a while, then walk around. A friend of mine paces the floor of his room for his prayer time. Rather than get cramped in one position, take a walk and stretch; get some variety.

As outside things pop into your mind,

simply incorporate those items into prayer. If it's some business item you must not forget, jot it down. Have you noticed how many things come to mind while you are sitting in church? It will be natural for things to occur to you during your prayer day that you should have done, so put them down, pray about them and plan how you can take care of them and when. Don't just push them aside or they will plague you the rest of the day.

At the end of the day summarize in your notebook some things God has spoken to you about. This will be profitable to refer to later.

Two Questions

The result of your day of prayer should be answers to the two questions Paul asked the Lord on the Damascus road (Acts 22:6-10). Paul's first question was, "Who are you, Lord?" The Lord replied, "I am Jesus." You will be seeking to know Him, to find out who He is. The second question Paul asked was, "What shall I do, Lord?" The Lord answered him specifically. This should be answered or reconfirmed for you in that part of the day when you unhurriedly seek His will for you.

Don't think you must end the day with some new discovery or extraordinary experience. Wait on God and expose yourself to His Word. Looking for a new experience or insight you can share with someone when you get back will get you off the track. True, you may gain some new insight, but often this can just take your attention from the real business. The test of such a day is not how exhilarated we are when the day is over but how it works into life tomorrow. If we have really exposed ourselves to the Word and come into contact with God, it will affect our daily life.

Days of prayer don't just happen. Besides the attempts of our enemy Satan to keep us from praying, the world around us has plenty to offer to fill our time. So we have to *make* time. Plan ahead—the first of every other month, or once a quarter.

God bless you as you do this—and do it soon! You too will probably ask yourself, "Why not more often?"

"I love the LORD, for he heard my voice;
　he heard my cry for mercy.
Because he turned his ear to me,
　I will call on him as long as I live. . . .
I will sacrifice a thank offering to you
　and call on the name of the LORD."
　　　　　　　　　　—Psalm 116:1-2,17

Why a Day in Prayer?

Notes from your group discussion

1. FOR EXTENDED FELLOWSHIP WITH GOD

_____

_____

_____

_____

2. FOR A RENEWED PERSPECTIVE

_____

_____

_____

_____

_____

3. FOR ADDITIONAL INTERCESSION

_____

_____

_____

_____

_____

4. FOR PERSONAL INVENTORY AND EVALUATION

_____

_____

_____

_____

_____

5. FOR ADEQUATE PREPARATION

_____

_____

_____

_____

Divide the Day into Three Parts

1. **WAIT ON THE LORD**
   a. To realize His presence.
   b. To be cleansed.
   c. To worship Him.

2. **PRAY FOR OTHERS**
   a. Ask specific things for them.
   b. Use Paul's prayers for others.
   c. Ask for others what you are praying for yourself.

3. **PRAY FOR YOURSELF**
   a. Guidance and wisdom.
   b. Godliness.
   c. Concerns and needs.

How to Stay Awake and Alert

1. Get adequate rest the two nights before your day in prayer.
2. Change positions—sit a while, walk around, etc.
3. Have a variety in what you do. Read the Scriptures a while, pray a while, plan or organize a while, and so on.
4. Pray aloud—in a whisper or soft voice. Sometimes thinking aloud also helps.

How to Make a Worry List

Problems and concerns can sometimes preoccupy our minds. Preparing a worry list can help to free us from the distraction of our concerns and help us move toward their resolution. Try the following suggestions in preparing your own worry list.

1. Give some thought to current conflicts, problems, concerns, or frustrations. List anything that is "bugging" you. Number each of these items. No matter how small an item is, if it is of concern to you, list it. Ask God to reveal to you anything else which is a point of concern.
2. Every worry that you have in the world should be on that piece of paper. Nothing else should concern you—it is all there! When you are satisfied that all of your concerns have been listed, go on to step 3.
3. Go through the list item by item. On each item you will conclude that you can do nothing about it because it is past or beyond your control, or that you can do something to resolve that issue.

If there is nothing you can do about a given item, then spend some time in prayer about it. If you feel that you can take action on a particular item, you should also pray about it, then make a "do list" of things you plan to do specifically to help resolve it. After you have gone through many of these concerns, you will have several items on a "do list."

As a result of your day in prayer, you will also come up with other things which should go on this "do list."

4. You may want to dispose of your "worry list" if it has some rather personal or pointed items which could be embarrassing or awkward if others were to read them.

It is not uncommon for an individual to have around 20 items on a "worry list" when it is compiled on a monthly basis.

A Checklist for a Day in Prayer

1. ESSENTIAL
a. A Bible—perhaps the one you read regularly
b. A notebook or paper for taking notes
c. Pens or pencils
d. A clock or watch

2. OPTIONAL
a. Prayer letters from missionaries and Christian workers
b. A devotional book such as:
   (1) *Power through Prayer* by E.M. Bounds
   (2) *Words to Winners of Souls* by Horatius Bonar
   (3) *Prayer—Conversing with God* by Rosalind Rinker
   (4) *The Practice of the Presence of God* by Brother Lawrence
   (5) *Pray: How to be Effective in Prayer* by Warren and Ruth Myers
   (6) *Purpose in Prayer* by E.M. Bounds
c. A bag lunch and beverage
d. Your current prayer list
e. Memory cards—to put in some extra review and meditation time or to pray about these verses
f. Your *Bible Reading Highlights Record* for recent months—to look for trends in God's dealing with you
g. Comfortable clothing
h. A calendar of the months ahead
i. A hymn book
j. Notes from your last day in prayer
k. Your list of objectives or goals
l. Facts about a decision you are making
m. A copy of your weekly schedule

Sample: How to Take Notes During a Half Day in Prayer

1:15–1:45	John 14-16	30 min.
	14:3 Heaven is still being prepared	
	14:13 Jesus' involvement in prayer	
	14:15,21 Obey !! (15:7,10)	
	16:26 "Then you shall present your petitions over	
	my signature."	
1:45–1:50	Confession time	5 min.
1:50–2:00	Reviewing "How to Spend a Day in Prayer"	10 min.
2:00–2:15	Psa.145- Reading, Praise, Worship	15 min.
	145:3,6 We have a great God !!	
	145:4 He will work with my children	
	145:9 I'm thankful for God's mercy !	
	145:15 God meets needs—He has met mine !	
	145:17 I want to grow in holiness	
2:15–3:00	Making a "Worry List" (prayer and do list)	45 min.
3:00–3:20	Prayer for other people	20 min.

Do List :

   1. Organize prayer sheets

   2. Apologize to_____ about_____

   3. Clean out car trunk

4:00–4:20	Conclusions	20 min.

   1. Quiet time and memory review must be daily

   things I "never" miss!

   2. Pray and work towards a balanced life !!

ASSIGNMENT FOR SESSION 11

1. Scripture Memory: No new verses are assigned for next time. Spend some time perfecting the verses you learned in *Growing Strong In God's Family* and in this course.
2. Quiet Time: Continue reading, marking and recording.
3. Other:
   a. Come rested, alert and eager to spend a half day with the Lord. Carefully look over the checklist on page 85.
   b. Work on getting all requirements done for Course 1 and your *Completion Record* signed off.

Session 11

OUTLINE OF THIS SESSION:
1. Meet together for a brief orientation (10 minutes or less).
2. Scatter and spend individual time alone with God (3 hours and 20 minutes).
3. Come back together again to share what you have done during your time alone and your observations on this experience (30 minutes).

The Challenge Continues . . .

In this first course of *The 2:7 Series* you have further developed your walk with Christ by:
- Learning how to prepare and present your personal testimony of Christ's work in your life;
- Learning how to spend extended periods of time alone with God, and spending a half day in prayer;
- Reading about and discussing how Christ must be the Lord of our lives;
- Memorizing 12 key verses on critically important aspects of a balanced Christian life;
- Studying scriptural principles for walking with Christ.

In Course 2 you will find more challenges to deepening your Christian life. You will continue your growth by:
- Learning how to meditate on the Scriptures;
- Learning how to use *The Bridge Illustration* to communicate the gospel;
- Memorizing 12 key verses to use in presenting the gospel;
- Studying key aspects of The Character of the Christian.

Notes

PAGE	SOURCE
32	Basil Miller, *George Mueller, Man of Faith* (Minneapolis: Bethany Fellowship, Inc., 1972).
32	Andrew Murray, *The New Life* (Minneapolis: Bethany Fellowship, Inc., 1965).
38	Paul Little, *Affirming the Will of God* (Downers Grove, Illinois: InterVarsity Press 1971).
44	Ole Hallesby, *Prayer* (Minneapolis: Augsburg Publishing House, 1975).
46	J. Oswald Sanders, *Spiritual Leadership* (Chicago: Moody Press, 1967).

BIBLE READING HIGHLIGHTS RECORD

"Happy are those who keep My ways. Hear instruction and be wise, and do not refuse it. Happy is the man listening to Me, watching daily at My gates, keeping watch at My doorposts."

Proverbs 8:32-34, BERK

*Translation*_____ *Year*_____

○ **Sunday**   Date_____ All I read today_____
Best thing I marked today: *Reference:*_____
Thought: _____
_____
_____
How it impressed me:_____
_____
_____
_____
_____
_____
_____

○ **Monday**   Date_____ All I read today_____
Best thing I marked today: *Reference:*_____
Thought: _____
_____
_____
How it impressed me:_____
_____
_____
_____
_____
_____
_____

○ **Tuesday**   Date_____ All I read today_____
Best thing I marked today: *Reference:*_____
Thought: _____
_____
_____
How it impressed me:_____
_____
_____
_____
_____

○ **Wednesday** Date_____ All I read today_____
Best thing I marked today: *Reference:*_____
Thought: _____
_____
_____
_____
How it impressed me:_____
_____
_____
_____
_____
_____
_____
_____

○ **Thursday** Date_____ All I read today_____
Best thing I marked today: *Reference:*_____
Thought: _____
_____
_____
How it impressed me:_____
_____
_____
_____
_____
_____
_____

○ **Friday**   Date_____ All I read today_____
Best thing I marked today: *Reference:*_____
Thought: _____
_____
_____
How it impressed me:_____
_____
_____
_____
_____
_____
_____

○ **Saturday** Date_____ All I read today_____
Best thing I marked today: *Reference:*_____
Thought: _____
_____
_____
How it impressed me:_____
_____
_____
_____
_____

BIBLE READING HIGHLIGHTS RECORD

"Happy are those who keep My ways. Hear instruction and be wise, and do not refuse it. Happy is the man listening to Me, watching daily at My gates, keeping watch at My doorposts."

Proverbs 8:32-34, BERK

*Translation*_____ *Year* _____

○ **Sunday** Date_____ All I read today_____
Best thing I marked today: *Reference:*_____
*Thought:*_____
_____
_____
How it impressed me:_____
_____
_____
_____
_____
_____
_____
_____

○ **Monday** Date_____ All I read today_____
Best thing I marked today: *Reference:*_____
*Thought:*_____
_____
_____
How it impressed me:_____
_____
_____
_____
_____
_____
_____
_____

○ **Tuesday** Date_____ All I read today_____
Best thing I marked today: *Reference:*_____
*Thought:*_____
_____
_____
How it impressed me:_____
_____
_____
_____
_____
_____

○ **Wednesday** Date_____ All I read today_____
Best thing I marked today: *Reference:*_____
*Thought:*_____
_____
_____
_____
How it impressed me:_____
_____
_____
_____
_____
_____
_____
_____
_____
_____
_____

○ **Thursday** Date_____ All I read today_____
Best thing I marked today: *Reference:*_____
*Thought:*_____
_____
_____
How it impressed me:_____
_____
_____
_____
_____
_____
_____
_____

○ **Friday** Date_____ All I read today_____
Best thing I marked today: *Reference:*_____
*Thought:*_____
_____
_____
How it impressed me:_____
_____
_____
_____
_____
_____
_____
_____

○ **Saturday** Date_____ All I read today_____
Best thing I marked today: *Reference:*_____
*Thought:*_____
_____
_____
How it impressed me:_____
_____
_____
_____
_____
_____

BIBLE READING HIGHLIGHTS RECORD

"Happy are those who keep My ways. Hear instruction and be wise, and do not refuse it. Happy is the man listening to Me, watching daily at My gates, keeping watch at My doorposts."

Proverbs 8:32-34, BERK

*Translation*_____ *Year* _____

○ **Sunday**   Date_____ All I read today_____
Best thing I marked today: *Reference:*_____
Thought: _____
_____
_____
_____

How it impressed me:_____
_____
_____
_____
_____
_____
_____

○ **Monday**   Date_____ All I read today_____
Best thing I marked today: *Reference:*_____
Thought: _____
_____
_____
_____

How it impressed me:_____
_____
_____
_____
_____
_____
_____
_____

○ **Tuesday**   Date_____ All I read today_____
Best thing I marked today: *Reference:*_____
Thought: _____
_____
_____
_____

How it impressed me:_____
_____
_____
_____
_____
_____

○ **Wednesday** Date_____ All I read today_____
Best thing I marked today: *Reference:*_____
Thought: _____
_____
_____
_____

How it impressed me:_____
_____
_____
_____
_____
_____
_____
_____

○ **Thursday**   Date_____ All I read today_____
Best thing I marked today: *Reference:*_____
Thought: _____
_____
_____
_____

How it impressed me:_____
_____
_____
_____
_____
_____
_____

○ **Friday**   Date_____ All I read today_____
Best thing I marked today: *Reference:*_____
Thought: _____
_____
_____
_____

How it impressed me:_____
_____
_____
_____
_____

○ **Saturday**   Date_____ All I read today_____
Best thing I marked today: *Reference:*_____
Thought: _____
_____
_____

How it impressed me:_____
_____
_____
_____
_____

BIBLE READING HIGHLIGHTS RECORD

"Happy are those who keep My ways. Hear instruction and be wise, and do not refuse it. Happy is the man listening to Me, watching daily at My gates, keeping watch at My doorposts."

Proverbs 8:32-34, BERK

*Translation*_____ *Year* _____

◯ **Sunday**   Date_____ All I read today_____
Best thing I marked today: *Reference:*_____
Thought: _____
_____
_____
How it impressed me:_____
_____
_____
_____
_____
_____
_____

◯ **Monday**   Date_____ All I read today_____
Best thing I marked today: *Reference:*_____
Thought: _____
_____
_____
How it impressed me:_____
_____
_____
_____
_____
_____
_____
_____
_____

◯ **Tuesday**   Date_____ All I read today_____
Best thing I marked today: *Reference:*_____
Thought: _____
_____
_____
How it impressed me:_____
_____
_____
_____
_____
_____
_____

◯ **Wednesday** Date_____ All I read today_____
Best thing I marked today: *Reference:*_____
Thought: _____
_____
_____
_____
How it impressed me:_____
_____
_____
_____
_____
_____
_____
_____
_____

◯ **Thursday**   Date_____ All I read today_____
Best thing I marked today: *Reference:*_____
Thought: _____
_____
_____
How it impressed me:_____
_____
_____
_____
_____
_____
_____

◯ **Friday**   Date_____ All I read today_____
Best thing I marked today: *Reference:*_____
Thought: _____
_____
_____
How it impressed me:_____
_____
_____
_____
_____
_____
_____
_____

◯ **Saturday**   Date_____ All I read today_____
Best thing I marked today: *Reference:*_____
Thought: _____
_____
_____
How it impressed me:_____
_____
_____
_____
_____
◯ **Wednesday** Date_____ All I read today_____
Thought: _____
_____

BIBLE READING HIGHLIGHTS RECORD

"Happy are those who keep My ways. Hear instruction and be wise, and do not refuse it. Happy is the man listening to Me, watching daily at My gates, keeping watch at My doorposts."

Proverbs 8:32-34, BERK

*Translation*_____ *Year*_____

◯ **Sunday**   Date_____ All I read today_____
Best thing I marked today: *Reference:*_____
*Thought:*_____
_____
_____
_____
How it impressed me:_____
_____
_____
_____
_____
_____
_____
_____
_____

◯ **Monday**   Date_____ All I read today_____
Best thing I marked today: *Reference:*_____
*Thought:*_____
_____
_____
How it impressed me:_____
_____
_____
_____
_____
_____
_____
_____
_____

◯ **Tuesday**   Date_____ All I read today_____
Best thing I marked today: *Reference:*_____
*Thought:*_____
_____
_____
How it impressed me:_____
_____
_____
_____
_____
_____
_____

◯ **Wednesday** Date_____ All I read today_____
Best thing I marked today: *Reference:*_____
*Thought:*_____
_____
_____
_____
How it impressed me:_____
_____
_____
_____
_____
_____
_____
_____
_____

◯ **Thursday**   Date_____ All I read today_____
Best thing I marked today: *Reference:*_____
*Thought:*_____
_____
_____
How it impressed me:_____
_____
_____
_____
_____
_____
_____
_____

◯ **Friday**   Date_____ All I read today_____
Best thing I marked today: *Reference:*_____
*Thought:*_____
_____
_____
How it impressed me:_____
_____
_____
_____
_____
_____

◯ **Saturday**   Date_____ All I read today_____
Best thing I marked today: *Reference:*_____
*Thought:*_____
_____
How it impressed me:_____
_____
_____
_____

BIBLE READING HIGHLIGHTS RECORD

"Happy are those who keep My ways. Hear instruction and be wise, and do not refuse it. Happy is the man listening to Me, watching daily at My gates, keeping watch at My doorposts."

Proverbs 8:32-34, BERK

*Translation*_____ *Year*_____

○ **Sunday**   Date_____ All I read today_____
Best thing I marked today: *Reference:*_____
*Thought:*_____
_____
_____

How it impressed me:_____
_____
_____
_____
_____
_____
_____

○ **Monday**   Date_____ All I read today_____
Best thing I marked today: *Reference:*_____
*Thought:*_____
_____
_____

How it impressed me:_____
_____
_____
_____
_____
_____
_____

○ **Tuesday**   Date_____ All I read today_____
Best thing I marked today: *Reference:*_____
*Thought:*_____
_____
_____

How it impressed me:_____
_____
_____
_____
_____

○ **Wednesday** Date_____ All I read today_____
Best thing I marked today: *Reference:*_____
*Thought:*_____
_____
_____

How it impressed me:_____
_____
_____
_____
_____
_____
_____
_____
_____

○ **Thursday**   Date_____ All I read today_____
Best thing I marked today: *Reference:*_____
*Thought:*_____
_____
_____

How it impressed me:_____
_____
_____
_____
_____
_____
_____

○ **Friday**   Date_____ All I read today_____
Best thing I marked today: *Reference:*_____
*Thought:*_____
_____
_____

How it impressed me:_____
_____
_____
_____
_____
_____
_____

○ **Saturday**   Date_____ All I read today_____
Best thing I marked today: *Reference:*_____
*Thought:*_____
_____
_____

How it impressed me:_____
_____
_____
_____
_____

BIBLE READING HIGHLIGHTS RECORD

"Happy are those who keep My ways. Hear instruction and be wise, and do not refuse it. Happy is the man listening to Me, watching daily at My gates, keeping watch at My doorposts."

Proverbs 8:32-34, BERK

Translation_____ Year _____

○ **Sunday** Date_____ All I read today_____
Best thing I marked today: *Reference:*_____
Thought: _____
_____
_____
How it impressed me:_____
_____
_____
_____
_____
_____
_____
_____
_____

○ **Monday** Date_____ All I read today_____
Best thing I marked today: *Reference:*_____
Thought: _____
_____
_____
How it impressed me:_____
_____
_____
_____
_____
_____
_____
_____
_____
_____

○ **Tuesday** Date_____ All I read today_____
Best thing I marked today: *Reference:*_____
Thought: _____
_____
_____
How it impressed me:_____
_____
_____
_____
_____
_____
_____

○ **Wednesday** Date_____ All I read today_____
Best thing I marked today: *Reference:*_____
Thought: _____
_____
_____
_____
_____
How it impressed me:_____
_____
_____
_____
_____
_____
_____
_____
_____
_____
_____

○ **Thursday** Date_____ All I read today_____
Best thing I marked today: *Reference:*_____
Thought: _____
_____
_____
How it impressed me:_____
_____
_____
_____
_____
_____
_____
_____
_____

○ **Friday** Date_____ All I read today_____
Best thing I marked today: *Reference:*_____
Thought: _____
_____
_____
How it impressed me:_____
_____
_____
_____
_____
_____
_____
_____
_____
_____

○ **Saturday** Date_____ All I read today_____
Best thing I marked today: *Reference:*_____
Thought: _____
_____
_____
_____
How it impressed me:_____
_____
_____
_____
_____
_____
_____

BIBLE READING HIGHLIGHTS RECORD

"Happy are those who keep My ways. Hear instruction and be wise, and do not refuse it. Happy is the man listening to Me, watching daily at My gates, keeping watch at My doorposts."

Proverbs 8:32-34, BERK

*Translation*_____ *Year*_____

Sunday Date_____ All I read today_____
Best thing I marked today: *Reference:*_____
*Thought:*_____
_____
_____
_____
How it impressed me:_____
_____
_____
_____
_____
_____
_____
_____

Monday Date_____ All I read today_____
Best thing I marked today: *Reference:*_____
*Thought:*_____
_____
_____
_____
How it impressed me:_____
_____
_____
_____
_____
_____
_____
_____

Tuesday Date_____ All I read today_____
Best thing I marked today: *Reference:*_____
*Thought:*_____
_____
_____
How it impressed me:_____
_____
_____
_____
_____
_____
_____

Wednesday Date_____ All I read today_____
Best thing I marked today: *Reference:*_____
*Thought:*_____
_____
_____
_____
How it impressed me:_____
_____
_____
_____
_____
_____
_____
_____
_____
_____
_____

Thursday Date_____ All I read today_____
Best thing I marked today: *Reference:*_____
*Thought:*_____
_____
_____
How it impressed me:_____
_____
_____
_____
_____
_____
_____
_____

Friday Date_____ All I read today_____
Best thing I marked today: *Reference:*_____
*Thought:*_____
_____
_____
How it impressed me:_____
_____
_____
_____
_____
_____
_____

Saturday Date_____ All I read today_____
Best thing I marked today: *Reference:*_____
*Thought:*_____
_____
_____
How it impressed me:_____
_____
_____
_____
_____
_____
_____

BIBLE READING HIGHLIGHTS RECORD

"Happy are those who keep My ways. Hear instruction and be wise, and do not refuse it. Happy is the man listening to Me, watching daily at My gates, keeping watch at My doorposts."

Proverbs 8:32-34, BERK

Translation_____ Year _____

○ **Sunday**   Date_____ All I read today_____
Best thing I marked today: *Reference:*_____
Thought: _____
_____
_____
How it impressed me:_____
_____
_____
_____
_____
_____
_____

○ **Monday**   Date_____ All I read today_____
Best thing I marked today: *Reference:*_____
Thought: _____
_____
_____
How it impressed me:_____
_____
_____
_____
_____
_____
_____

○ **Tuesday**   Date_____ All I read today_____
Best thing I marked today: *Reference:*_____
Thought: _____
_____
_____
How it impressed me:_____
_____
_____
_____
_____
_____
_____

○ **Wednesday** Date_____ All I read today_____
Best thing I marked today: *Reference:*_____
Thought: _____
_____
_____
_____
How it impressed me:_____
_____
_____
_____
_____
_____
_____
_____

○ **Thursday**   Date_____ All I read today_____
Best thing I marked today: *Reference:*_____
Thought: _____
_____
_____
How it impressed me:_____
_____
_____
_____
_____
_____

○ **Friday**   Date_____ All I read today_____
Best thing I marked today: *Reference:*_____
Thought: _____
_____
_____
How it impressed me:_____
_____
_____
_____
_____
_____

○ **Saturday**   Date_____ All I read today_____
Best thing I marked today: *Reference:*_____
Thought: _____
_____
_____
How it impressed me:_____
_____
_____
_____
_____
_____

BIBLE READING HIGHLIGHTS RECORD

"Happy are those who keep My ways. Hear instruction and be wise, and do not refuse it. Happy is the man listening to Me, watching daily at My gates, keeping watch at My doorposts."

Proverbs 8:32-34, BERK

Translation_____ Year _____

○ **Sunday**   Date_____ All I read today_____
Best thing I marked today: *Reference:*_____
Thought: _____
_____
_____
_____
How it impressed me:_____
_____
_____
_____
_____
_____
_____
_____
_____

○ **Monday**   Date_____ All I read today_____
Best thing I marked today: *Reference:*_____
Thought: _____
_____
_____
_____
How it impressed me:_____
_____
_____
_____
_____
_____
_____
_____
_____

○ **Tuesday**   Date_____ All I read today_____
Best thing I marked today: *Reference:*_____
Thought: _____
_____
_____
How it impressed me:_____
_____
_____
_____
_____
_____
_____

○ **Wednesday** Date_____ All I read today_____
Best thing I marked today: *Reference:*_____
Thought: _____
_____
_____
_____
How it impressed me:_____
_____
_____
_____
_____
_____
_____
_____
_____
_____
_____

○ **Thursday**   Date_____ All I read today_____
Best thing I marked today: *Reference:*_____
Thought: _____
_____
_____
_____
How it impressed me:_____
_____
_____
_____
_____
_____
_____
_____

○ **Friday**   Date_____ All I read today_____
Best thing I marked today: *Reference:*_____
Thought: _____
_____
_____
_____
How it impressed me:_____
_____
_____
_____
_____
_____
_____
_____

○ **Saturday**   Date_____ All I read today_____
Best thing I marked today: *Reference:*_____
Thought: _____
_____
_____
How it impressed me:_____
_____
_____
_____
_____
_____
_____

BIBLE READING HIGHLIGHTS RECORD

"Happy are those who keep My ways. Hear instruction and be wise, and do not refuse it. Happy is the man listening to Me, watching daily at My gates, keeping watch at My doorposts."

Proverbs 8:32-34, BERK

Translation_____ Year _____

Sunday Date_____ All I read today_____
Best thing I marked today: *Reference:*_____
Thought: _____
_____
_____
_____
How it impressed me:_____
_____
_____
_____
_____
_____
_____
_____

Monday Date_____ All I read today_____
Best thing I marked today: *Reference:*_____
Thought: _____
_____
_____
How it impressed me:_____
_____
_____
_____
_____
_____
_____
_____

Tuesday Date_____ All I read today_____
Best thing I marked today: *Reference:*_____
Thought: _____
_____
_____
How it impressed me:_____
_____
_____
_____
_____
_____

Wednesday Date_____ All I read today_____
Best thing I marked today: *Reference:*_____
Thought: _____
_____
_____
_____
How it impressed me:_____
_____
_____
_____
_____
_____
_____
_____
_____

Thursday Date_____ All I read today_____
Best thing I marked today: *Reference:*_____
Thought: _____
_____
_____
How it impressed me:_____
_____
_____
_____
_____
_____
_____

Friday Date_____ All I read today_____
Best thing I marked today: *Reference:*_____
Thought: _____
_____
_____
How it impressed me:_____
_____
_____
_____
_____
_____
_____
_____

Saturday Date_____ All I read today_____
Best thing I marked today: *Reference:*_____
Thought: _____
_____
_____
How it impressed me:_____
_____
_____
_____

BIBLE READING HIGHLIGHTS RECORD

"Happy are those who keep My ways. Hear instruction and be wise, and do not refuse it. Happy is the man listening to Me, watching daily at My gates, keeping watch at My doorposts."

Proverbs 8:32-34, BERK

*Translation*_____ *Year*_____

○ **Sunday**   Date_____ All I read today_____
Best thing I marked today: *Reference:*_____
*Thought:*_____
_____
_____
_____

How it impressed me:_____
_____
_____
_____
_____
_____
_____
_____

○ **Monday**   Date_____ All I read today_____
Best thing I marked today: *Reference:*_____
*Thought:*_____
_____
_____
_____

How it impressed me:_____
_____
_____
_____
_____
_____
_____
_____

○ **Tuesday**   Date_____ All I read today_____
Best thing I marked today: *Reference:*_____
*Thought:*_____
_____
_____

How it impressed me:_____
_____
_____
_____
_____
_____

○ **Wednesday** Date_____ All I read today_____
Best thing I marked today: *Reference:*_____
*Thought:*_____
_____
_____
_____
_____

How it impressed me:_____
_____
_____
_____
_____
_____
_____
_____
_____

○ **Thursday**   Date_____ All I read today_____
Best thing I marked today: *Reference:*_____
*Thought:*_____
_____
_____

How it impressed me:_____
_____
_____
_____
_____
_____
_____
_____

○ **Friday**   Date_____ All I read today_____
Best thing I marked today: *Reference:*_____
*Thought:*_____
_____
_____

How it impressed me:_____
_____
_____
_____
_____
_____

○ **Saturday**   Date_____ All I read today_____
Best thing I marked today: *Reference:*_____
*Thought:*_____
_____
_____

How it impressed me:_____
_____
_____
_____
_____
_____

Prayer Sheet

REQUEST	GOD'S ANSWER

Prayer Sheet

REQUEST	GOD'S ANSWER

Christit the Center
NIV

2 Corinthians 5:17

Therefore, if anyone is in Christ, he is a new creation; the old has gone, the new has come!

2 Corinthians 5:17

Christ the Center
NIV

Galatians 2:20

I have been crucified with Christ and I no longer live, but Christ lives in me. The life I live in the body, I live by faith in the Son of God, who loved me and gave himself for me.

Galatians 2:20

Obedience to Christ
NIV

Romans 12:1

Therefore, I urge you, brothers, in view of God's mercy, to offer your bodies as living sacrifices, holy and pleasing to God—this is your spiritual act of worship.

Romans 12:1

Obedience to Christ
NIV

John 14:21

"Whoever has my commands and obeys them, he is the one who loves me. He who loves me will be loved by my Father, and I too will love him and show myself to him."

John 14:21

The Word
NIV

2 Timothy 3:16

All Scripture is God-breathed and is useful for teaching, rebuking, correcting and training in righteousness.

2 Timothy 3:16

The Word
NIV

Joshua 1:8

"Do not let this Book of the Law depart from your mouth; meditate on it day and night, so that you may be careful to do everything written in it. Then you will be prosperous and successful."

Joshua 1:8

Prayer
NIV

John 15:7

"If you remain in me and my words remain in you, ask whatever you wish, and it will be given you."

John 15:7

Prayer
NIV

Philippians 4:6-7

Do not be anxious about anything, but in everything, by prayer and petition, with thanksgiving, present your requests to God. And the peace of God, which transcends all understanding, will guard your hearts and your minds in Christ Jesus.

Philippians 4:6-7

Fellowship
NIV

1 John 1:3

We proclaim to you what we have seen and heard, so that you also may have fellowship with us. And our fellowship is with the Father and with his Son, Jesus Christ.

1 John 1:3

Fellowship
NIV

Hebrews 10:24-25

And let us consider how we may spur one another on toward love and good deeds. Let us not give up meeting together, as some are in the habit of doing, but let us encourage one another—and all the more as you see the Day approaching.

Hebrews 10:24-25

Witnessing
NIV

Matthew 4:19

"Come, follow me," Jesus said, "and I will make you fishers of men."

Matthew 4:19

Witnessing
NIV

Romans 1:16

I am not ashamed of the gospel, because it is the power of God for the salvation of everyone who believes: first for the Jew, then for the Gentile.

Romans 1:16

Christh the Center
KJV

2 Corinthians 5:17

Therefore if any man be in Christ, he is a new creature: old things are passed away; behold, all things are become new.

2 Corinthians 5:17 ·

A-1   Live the New Life

Christ the Center
KJV

Galatians 2:20

I am crucified with Christ: nevertheless I live; yet not I, but Christ liveth in me: and the life which I now live in the flesh I live by the faith of the Son of God, who loved me, and gave himself for me.

Galatians 2:20

A-2   Live the New Life

Obedience to Christ
KJV

Romans 12:1

I beseech you therefore, brethren, by the mercies of God, that ye present your bodies a living sacrifice, holy, acceptable unto God, which is your reasonable service.

Romans 12:1

A-3   Live the New Life

Obedience to Christ
KJV

John 14:21

He that hath my commandments, and keepeth them, he it is that loveth me: and he that loveth me shall be loved of my Father, and I will love him, and will manifest myself to him.

John 14:21

A-4   Live the New Life

The Word
KJV

2 Timothy 3:16

All Scripture is given by inspiration of God, and is profitable for doctrine, for reproof, for correction, for instruction in righteousness.

2 Timothy 3:16

A-5   Live the New Life

The Word
KJV

Joshua 1:8

This book of the law shall not depart out of thy mouth; but thou shalt meditate therein day and night, that thou mayest observe to do according to all that is written therein: for then thou shalt make thy way prosperous, and then thou shalt have good success.

Joshua 1:8

A-6   Live the New Life

Prayer
KJV

John 15:7

If ye abide in me, and my words abide in you, ye shall ask what ye will, and it shall be done unto you.

John 15:7

A-7   Live the New Life

Prayer
KJV

Philippians 4:6-7

Be careful for nothing; but in every thing by prayer and supplication with thanksgiving let your requests be made known unto God. And the peace of God, which passeth all understanding, shall keep your hearts and minds through Christ Jesus.

Philippians 4:6-7

A-8   Live the New Life

Fellowship
KJV

1 John 1:3

That which we have seen and heard declare we unto you, that ye also may have fellowship with us: and truly our fellowship is with the Father, and with his Son Jesus Christ.

1 John 1:3

A-9   Live the New Life

Fellowship
KJV

Hebrews 10:24-25

And let us consider one another to provoke unto love and to good works: not forsaking the assembling of ourselves together, as the manner of some is; but exhorting one another: and so much the more as ye see the day approaching.

Hebrews 10:24-25

A-10   Live the New Live

Witnessing
KJV

Matthew 4:19

And he saith unto them, Follow me, and I will make you fishers of men.

Matthew 4:19

A-11   Live the New Life

Witnessing
KJV

Romans 1:16

For I am not ashamed of the gospel of Christ: for it is the power of God unto salvation to every one that believeth; to the Jew first, and also to the Greek.

Romans 1:16

A-12   Live the New Life

Christus the Center — RSV

Christ the Center   RSV

2 Corinthians 5:17

Therefore, if anyone is in Christ, he is a new creation; the old has passed away, behold, the new has come.

2 Corinthians 5:17

Christ the Center   RSV

Galatians 2:20

I have been crucified with Christ; it is no longer I who live, but Christ who lives in me; and the life I now live in the flesh I live by faith in the Son of God, who loved me and gave himself for me.

Galatians 2:20

Obedience to Christ   RSV

Romans 12:1

I appeal to you therefore, brethren, by the mercies of God, to present your bodies as a living sacrifice, holy and acceptable to God, which is your spiritual worship.

Romans 12:1

Obedience to Christ   RSV

John 14:21

"He who has my commandments and keeps them, he it is who loves me; and he who loves me will be loved by my Father, and I will love him and manifest myself to him."

John 14:21

The Word   RSV

2 Timothy 3:16

All scripture is inspired by God and profitable for teaching, for reproof, for correction, and for training in righteousness.

2 Timothy 3:16

The Word   RSV

Joshua 1:8

"This book of the law shall not depart out of your mouth, but you shall meditate on it day and night, that you may be careful to do according to all that is written in it; for then you shall make your way prosperous, and then you shall have good success."

Joshua 1:8

Prayer   RSV

John 15:7

"If you abide in me, and my words abide in you, ask whatever you will, and it shall be done for you."

John 15:7

Prayer   RSV

Philippians 4:6-7

Have no anxiety about anything, but in everything by prayer and supplication with thanksgiving let your requests be made known to God. And the peace of God, which passes all understanding, will keep your hearts and your minds in Christ Jesus.

Philippians 4:6-7

Fellowship   RSV

1 John 1:3

That which we have seen and heard we proclaim also to you, so that you may have fellowship with us; and our fellowship is with the Father and with his Son Jesus Christ.

1 John 1:3

Fellowship   RSV

Hebrews 10:24-25

And let us consider how to stir up one another to love and good works, not neglecting to meet together, as is the habit of some, but encouraging one another, and all the more as you see the Day drawing near.

Hebrews 10:24-25

Witnessing   RSV

Matthew 4:19

And he said to them, "Follow me, and I will make you fishers of men."

Matthew 4:19

Witnessing   RSV

Romans 1:16

For I am not ashamed of the gospel: it is the power of God for salvation to every one who has faith, to the Jew first and also to the Greek.

Romans 1:16

Christ the Center NASB

2 Corinthians 5:17

Therefore if any man is in Christ, he is a new creature; the old things passed away; behold, new things have come.

2 Corinthians 5:17

A-1 Live the New Life

Christ the Center NASB

Galatians 2:20

I have been crucified with Christ; and it is no longer I who live, but Christ lives in me; and the life which I now live in the flesh I live by faith in the Son of God, who loved me, and delivered Himself up for me.

Galatians 2:20

A-2 Live the New Life

Obedience to Christ NASB

Romans 12:1

I urge you therefore, brethren, by the mercies of God, to present your bodies a living and holy sacrifice, acceptable to God, which is your spiritual service of worship.

Romans 12:1

A-3 Live the New Life

Obedience to Christ NASB

John 14:21

"He who has My commandments, and keeps them, he it is who loves Me; and he who loves Me shall be loved by My Father, and I will love him, and will disclose Myself to him."

John 14:21

A-4 Live the New Life

The Word NASB

2 Timothy 3:16

All Scripture is inspired by God and profitable for teaching, for reproof, for correction, for training in righteousness.

2 Timothy 3:16

A-5 Live the New Life

The Word NASB

Joshua 1:8

"This book of the law shall not depart from your mouth, but you shall meditate on it day and night, so that you may be careful to do according to all that is written in it; for then you will make your way prosperous, and then you will have success."

Joshua 1:8

A-6 Live the New Life

Prayer NASB

John 15:7

"If you abide in Me, and My words abide in you, ask whatever you wish, and it shall be done for you."

John 15:7

A-7 Live the New Life

Prayer NASB

Philippians 4:6-7

Be anxious for nothing, but in everything by prayer and supplication with thanksgiving let your requests be made known to God. And the peace of God, which surpasses all comprehension, shall guard your hearts and your minds in Christ Jesus.

Philippians 4:6-7

A-8 Live the New Life

Fellowship NASB

1 John 1:3

What we have seen and heard we proclaim to you also, that you also may have fellowship with us; and indeed our fellowship is with the Father, and with His Son Jesus Christ.

1 John 1:3

A-9 Live the New Life

Fellowship NASB

Hebrews 10:24-25

And let us consider how to stimulate one another to love and good deeds, not forsaking our own assembling together, as is the habit of some, but encouraging one another; and all the more, as you see the day drawing near.

Hebrews 10:24-25

A-10 Live the New Life

Witnessing NASB

Matthew 4:19

And He said to them, "Follow Me, and I will make you fishers of men."

Matthew 4:19

A-11 Live the New Life

Witnessing NASB

Romans 1:16

For I am not ashamed of the gospel, for it is the power of God for salvation to every one who believes, to the Jew first and also to the Greek.

Romans 1:16

A-12 Live the New Life